SEVEN SECRETS
OF THE SAVVY
SCHOOL LEADER

SEVEN SECRETS OF THE SAVVY SCHOOL LEADER

A Guide to Surviving and Thriving

ROBERT EVANS

JOSSEY-BASS
A Wiley Imprint
www.josseybass.com

Published by Jossey-Bass
A Wiley Imprint
989 Market Street, San Francisco, CA 94103-1741—www.josseybass.com

Jossey-Bass books and products are available through most bookstores. To contact Jossey-Bass directly call our Customer Care Department within the U.S. at 800-956-7739, outside the U.S. at 317-572-3986, or fax 317-572-4002.

Jossey-Bass also publishes its books in a variety of electronic formats. Some content that appears in print may not be available in electronic books.

Library of Congress Cataloging-in-Publication Data
Evans, Robert, 1944-
  Seven secrets of the savvy school leader : a guide to surviving and thriving / Robert Evans.
    p. cm.
  Includes bibliographical references and index.
  ISBN 978-0-470-50732-2 (cloth)
  1. Educational leadership. 2. School management and organization. I. Title.
  LB2806.E87 2010
  371.2--dc22

                                    2009044802

Printed in the United States of America

FIRST EDITION

HB Printing   10 9 8 7 6 5 4 3 2 1

Contents

To Norm Colb and Keith Shahan
Savvy leaders, generous readers,
abiding friends.

Introduction

AMERICA'S SCHOOLS ARE FACING A NEW KIND OF CRISIS in leadership: almost no one, it seems, wants the job. For several decades now we have had much talk about a school leadership crisis, by which we meant a crisis of competence. We were convinced that our principals and superintendents needed to be more skilled, better trained, masters of turnaround and transformation. But the challenge is no longer just how to inspire and pressure them to perform, it is how to find—and keep—successors as they leave. An entire generation of leaders is retiring, many of them early, and the number of candidates applying to replace them is plummeting. So, too, is the tenure of their successors. In many districts, applications have shrunk by nearly two-thirds; in some states nearly half of those who do become principals leave their jobs within five years. Nor is the hiring challenge limited to public schools. In the independent school world, candidate pools for headships have also dropped sharply.

This collapse highlights an enormous irony about school leadership: it would appear that we have never known more about it than we do today, yet school leaders at all levels have never felt more stressed and vulnerable. For years now, most of the administrators I've met have said they love education, like leading, and can't imagine doing anything else, but that their quality of life has been deteriorating. Their jobs are, if not eating them up, eating into their lives. They are working harder than ever, longer than ever, dealing with ever greater complexity, sacrificing ever more of their personal and family time to their work. Despite this, they report, they are subject to ever more criticism and second-guessing and unrealistic expectations. They face two key sets of issues. The first is professional: Can I do it all? Can I master all that is now demanded of me? The second is personal: What does it take out of me to do it all? Is it worth it? Can I keep this up? Too many are answering with their feet.

This is a short book about the real-life dilemmas of being a school leader. Its focus is on the intersection of the professional and the personal in the lives of educational leaders. It is selective, not comprehensive; plain, not elaborate. It is not about how to become a heroic turnaround change agent, although it is very relevant to those contemplating such a role. It offers lots of specifics, but it is about taking perspective as much as it is about taking action. I hope to provide a context for rethinking school leadership, for reemphasizing its fundamentals, and in so doing, to simplify it. Most of what these pages propose truly is simple—not always easy by any means, but simple.

And almost none of it is truly secret. Despite the book's title, the concepts it shares are not hidden or hitherto unknown. They could equally be called truths, keys, or basics. Some could also be called practices, others perceptions. They are secrets in the sense that they are essential, that they lie at the core of leading well and of surviving the rigors of leading. And of course there are more than seven. The seven are the big headings, the organizing principles. Each subsumes a number of specific points, which the book examines. They include things to do, things to avoid, and expectations to reset. Although the book's focus throughout is on the real-life issues confronting leaders, it moves back and forth between describing daily, nitty-gritty practicalities and exploring the larger underlying context within which schools and leaders live.

Not only are these points not secret, they are not all mine alone. I have distilled them, drawing on the work of other writers and especially on my experience working with leaders of more than twelve hundred schools as well as other organizations over the past thirty years. My best teachers have been the principals, superintendents, school heads, and other leaders whom I think of as savvy. Savvy, to me, means having a practical, problem-solving wisdom, a general capacity to "handle things." It includes intangibles like having a good nose for problems, being able to read people, and knowing what makes a good solution to a dilemma. Savvy is a product of professional experience, learned skills that come with years of practice, but also of life experience, native intelligence, and common sense. It is one part of what I call authentic leadership. Its companion is integrity, a fundamental consistency between one's values, goals, and actions, a willingness to preach what one believes and practice what one preaches. Although my emphasis is on savvy, I will return at key moments to integrity and to authenticity, which are essential to inspiring commitment and performance.

I have long believed that the future of education in America depends not on giving schools and educators more to do but on making schooling—especially the leading of schools—more doable. The trends of recent years have been extraordinarily hard on school leaders. They have had to grapple with a vast unreasonable, punitive mandate (No Child Left Behind), and with many other initiatives, which, though more promising, have also made leadership more complex and less doable. My hope is that the secrets described in this book can help school leaders cope with the growing challenges they face, to be savvier and ultimately wiser—and thus to survive and thrive in their work and their lives.

Note: Throughout the book, endnote references simply identify sources, and contain no additional commentary.

Author's Note

IN THIS BOOK I RETURN TO TWO THEMES THAT HAVE BEEN enduring interests of mine and that I often think of as "leading and limits": the burdens and opportunities in school leadership and the need to understand schooling's impact in the full context of child development. Although much of what I present here is new, much is excerpted and adapted from my two previous books and from articles in which I've addressed these themes. In a different context and in different ways, I explored aspects of each of the seven secrets in *The Human Side of School Change* and in related articles. I draw on that work throughout this book, especially in Chapter Three and in parts of Chapters One, Two, and Five. But whereas my earlier interest was in the dynamics of change and their implications for leadership, here the subject is leadership itself, with implementing change as one of its dimensions.

More recently, I have concentrated on the challenges to schools and the limits on their influence caused by out-of-school factors, notably changes in the family. I examined these issues in *Family Matters: How Schools Can Cope with the Crisis in Childrearing* and in several companion articles. I draw on that work here, too, most directly in Chapter Four but also as a conceptual underpinning in Chapters Five, Six, and Seven.

Chapter One originally appeared, in slightly different form, in *Independent School* Spring 2009. A full list of my publications can be found at www.robevans.org.

SEVEN SECRETS
OF THE SAVVY
SCHOOL LEADER

The First Secret

When You Go to See the Wizard, Take Toto

America is a nation of believers, ready to place their faith in . . . workplace fads that inspire revivalist fervor, then fade away.

—Annie Murphy Paul[1]

L EADERS ALL OVER AMERICA KEEP SEARCHING FOR PEOPLE to tell them what to do. Like chronic dieters, anxious parents, eager investors, and earnest seekers of personal growth, they keep searching for the Answer, the Method, the Book, the Seminar—the key that will enable them to inspire their people and transform their organizations. Many make this a habit; they are perennially easy prey for the peddlers of miracle management cures. They are readily found in all fields and certainly in education. But there are exceptions, leaders whom I think of as savvy. Savvy school leaders don't seek serial saviors. They are often skeptics. They're not full-time skeptics and they're certainly not cynics, but they've learned to be wary of false prophets and promises. They, too, turn to gurus for advice, but rarely. And they know that whenever they do, they should, like Dorothy in *The Wizard of Oz*, take along a small terrier.

In the film classic, Dorothy, played by Judy Garland, is a Kansas farm girl who is transported to a magical land by a tornado and embarks on a quest to find the Wizard of Oz, hoping he can help her return home. She and her companions, the Tin Man, the Scarecrow, and the Cowardly Lion, find the Emerald City of Oz and reach the Wizard, but he refuses to help them until they bring him the broomstick of the Wicked Witch of the West. They do, but he still berates and bullies them until Toto, Dorothy's dog, tugs aside the curtain that hides him, revealing him to be nothing but an old man using tawdry magician's tricks and a microphone. Undone, he blusters, "Pay no attention to that man behind the curtain." But it's too late. The Wizard, they see, is a "humbug." A savvy leader could have told them.

America has produced a long line of management wizards. Over the past thirty years they have proliferated. Not all have been humbugs, but too many have been gross exaggerators. Many of their prescriptions have not only failed to fulfill their promises, they have turned out to be little more than passing fads. Although veteran educators often think of their field as uniquely prone to faddism—recurring cycles of "reform" in which old ideas keep returning with new names—corporate America is every bit as susceptible to the same phenomenon. Alas, there has been a growing tendency to import popular corporate leadership fads and models into education and to treat leadership itself as a kind of technology, a list of functions, techniques, and styles. These trends have been seductive to many, but the wisest school leaders have resisted them.

When More Is Less: Leadership Fads

It might seem that the knowledge base about leadership has never been greater. Countless books and articles have been published about it, including thousands about educational leadership alone. More corporate managers than ever have MBA degrees; more school administrators than ever have doctorates. Management is now widely seen as an applied science, and being an executive or administrator has come to mean acquiring and applying a body of theory and a set of skills. These skills are typically seen as portable: once versed in the proper techniques of structuring work and supervising people, and so on, leaders can employ these in a variety of settings: a bank, an insurance company, a hospital—or a school district.

Given all this, one might expect most of our companies, schools, and other organizations to be well run and the need for management advice books to decline. Not so. The books on leadership just keep multiplying. As Peter Vaill has noted, people everywhere continue to find their organizations "mysterious, recalcitrant, intractable, unpredictable, paradoxical, absurd, and—unless it's your own ox getting gored—funny."[2] Scott Adams continues to find fertile ground for his satire of organizational life in his Dilbert comic strip.

Good leadership remains as elusive as it is important; it still resists capture. In this it resembles Justice Potter Stewart's famous characterization of pornography: we know it when we see it, but it's extremely hard to define. Good leadership can be felt all through an organization, says Warren Bennis. In well-led organizations people feel that they make a significant contribution and that what they do has meaning; that they are part of a team or a family; that mastery and competence matter; that work is exciting and challenging.[3] In well-led organizations morale and commitment are high even in the face of hardship.

But though its impact is palpable, and though most of us feel we know a good leader when we meet one, the essence of leadership remains unclear. Is it a matter of skill or charisma? Of science or art? Of politics or principle? Are its methods universally applicable or situation-specific? Are leaders born or made? The answer to all these questions is, Yes. Leadership appears to be all these and more. Writing in 1985, Bennis and Bert Nanus noted that despite thousands of empirical studies yielding more than 850 definitions of leadership there was still no consensus about it. We still didn't know conclusively what distinguished leaders from nonleaders and strong leaders from weak ones.[4] More than twenty years later, we have even more studies and definitions, but are still no closer to a consensus.

This uncertainty has helped to sustain an enduring market for leadership fads and gurus. As they plan strategy and solve problems, leaders, especially those who want to be up to date, have a propensity to apply methods and techniques that are current in management circles. But as Matthew Stewart and other critics have observed, much of management theory, for all its claims to scientific and empirical gravitas, is essentially a kind of self-help literature. Like popular personal growth and parenting books, popular management and leadership books are faddish: they dress shallow and recycled advice in flashy new names; enjoy, in most cases, a relatively brief celebrity; then fade away. The fads succeed each other in a kind of carousel, Matthew Stewart says, emphasizing first one theme then another,[5] but none has proven to be an enduring silver bullet.

The gurus' flaws begin with selection bias—they typically generalize broadly from a narrow, hand-picked sample of leaders, describing a certain group of innovators who apparently succeeded using a particular approach or style. But this doesn't prove that all leaders who use this approach or style always succeed, no matter what circumstances they face (a caution that applies to some of the secrets this book recommends, as Chapter Five acknowledges). Similarly, the gurus often confuse correlation with causality. That employees of successful companies are happy, for example, doesn't prove that the companies succeeded because they made their employees happy; it may be that the employees are happy because the company is doing well.

More problematic is the gurus' tendency to adopt criteria for success that are simplistic and ignore or underplay the extent to which organizational success depends upon external factors that are unpredictable and unmanageable. Take, for example, Jim Collins, author of the runaway bestseller *Good to Great* and the dominant management wizard of the twenty-first century's first decade. Collins claimed to have avoided other gurus' methodological errors by, among other steps, analyzing a large range of companies to select eleven that qualified as leaping from good to great and by contrasting these with other similar companies that failed to make this leap. He claimed, too, that the factors he identified that led to their success were "immutable laws of organized human performance," and compared them to the laws of physics.[6]

But Collins's criterion for greatness could hardly have been shallower: stock price. He defined a great company as one whose stock outperformed the general market by three hundred percent over a fifteen-year period. Is stock price truly *the* proof of leadership and organizational excellence? Do well-led companies always fare well in the market, while poorly led companies always fare poorly? If so, how do we account for the fact that altering Collins's fifteen-year window by just a few months virtually eliminates his companies' exceptional stock performance?[7] Or for the fact that every one of his great companies saw its stock plummet during the 2008–2009 financial meltdown and that two of them, Fannie Mae and Circuit City, not only don't look great anymore, they look awful? Fannie Mae turned out to be abysmally led and was a major contributor to the subprime mortgage disaster that helped ravage the American economy; bailing it out is costing taxpayers billions. As for Circuit City, after being consistently outperformed by its rival Best Buy ever since *Good to Great* appeared, it went out of business. We can't expect Collins to have foreseen the collapse of the economy and its impact on stock prices. We can question his measure of leadership excellence. And we can note that an organization's fortunes—not just its failures but its successes—often depend not just on its leadership but on factors its leadership can neither anticipate nor control. (As Chapter Four will note, these kinds of factors loom especially large in schools.)

An equally serious flaw in the leadership fads, as Stewart points out, is not that the gurus' recommendations are so wrong but that so many are too right, "obvious in the extreme," as a principal friend of mine says. There is no harm in recommending simple or old truths—at least I hope not, as that's some of what this book does. It is something else again to pretend that these are new discoveries or to recommend empty truisms. Yet too often, as Stewart notes, the supposed experts offer a corporate version of the kind of "toothless wisdom" peddled by self-help writers—"quasi-religious dicta on the virtue of being good at what you do," illustrated by "parables (otherwise known as case studies)," and accompanied by exhortations that boil down to "Think harder!, Work smarter!" and the like.[8] Throughout, the gurus worship fervently and predictably at the altar of innovation, frequently with grandiose inanity. The field is littered with titles like *First Break All the Rules* and *The Pursuit of Wow!* and such pronouncements as "[Our approach] means re-thinking everything, everything!" and "Blow up [your own company] before the competition does."[9]

Finally, in addition to these weaknesses, the popular leadership fads typically have much less relevance to schools than to corporations. They are never developed in—or tailored to—educational settings. Nonetheless they are routinely foisted on school administrators. Since at least the 1980s there has been a predictable life cycle for a school leadership fad:

1. It begins outside of education, developed by management experts from studies of gifted business leaders or, occasionally, by political scientists from studies of gifted historical figures.

2. It gains favor in corporate America and becomes all the rage in management writing. Its key concepts and phrases ("thinking outside the box," "silos," "metrics," "benchmarking," "fox and hedgehog") become commonplace.

3. As it nears what later turns out to have been its peak of popularity, policymakers and professors of education

decide to apply it to schools, even if it has little apparent relevance there.

4. It heats up in educational circles as it cools in the corporate world, showing hitherto unnoticed weaknesses.

5. It is misapplied in education, either through slavish rigidity (failing to modify the model to fit schools' unique characteristics) or false clarity (adopting the nominal form of the innovation but not its true substance).

6. Well after it has lost its cachet in the business world, it lingers on in vestigial form in schools and schools of education until its popularity finally subsides there, too.

Remember Total Quality Management (TQM)? I have long cited it as a textbook example of this life cycle. It took corporate America by storm in the 1980s, and once this happened, it was inevitable that TQM would be applied to schools, even though some of its key concepts, such as "zero defects," simply aren't relevant there. About the time that its popularity began to accelerate in education, articles began to appear in the business press pointing out that TQM was not a panacea after all (among other things, it requires high levels of cooperation among employees, which can sag both when a company falls on hard times and layoffs loom and when employees' jobs are well protected and their motivation is low). Notions of "quality" and "continuous improvement," often ill-defined, are now enshrined in the leadership lexicon, but TQM itself soon lost its luster in management circles—and then finally in education. Collins's "good to great" approach has been enjoying the same status that TQM once did, but several years ago it started becoming popular among school leaders—superintendents and school heads across the country began having their boards read the book. This suggested to me that it might soon be waning in the corporate world. Sure enough, critics have begun pointing out the flaws noted above, as well as others in Collins's work.

The List of Functions Approach

Despite critiques like mine, there is broad agreement that management is, if not an applied science, a technical profession. Leading any kind of organization is widely understood to be, at least in good part, a learnable list of functions or skills. Researchers study successful managers and build an inventory of tasks or capacities (planning, budgeting, supervision, and so on) that are supposed to capture the essentials of the executive role. In education, the simplest version of this approach has been the following:

1. Find schools where pupils are achieving more than what might be predicted by their backgrounds.

2. Observe principals in those schools and find out what they are doing.

3. Identify these behaviors as "desirable traits."

4. Devise training programs to develop these traits in all principals.

5. Enlist principals in these programs.

This model, as Roland Barth has pointed out, is straightforward, compelling, logical—and surprisingly ineffective, because conditions in one school are seldom similar to those in another[10] and, as we shall see below, because few people can readily develop new traits and shed old ones.

A more complex version of this approach creates elaborate functional classifications. A typical example I came across years ago was a manual, *Principals for Our Changing Schools*. Its creators began with both a "task analysis of the principalship," results of which were reviewed by focus groups of administrators, and a "conceptual model and 'Taxonomy of Standards'" developed by academics. It then integrated the two, had this composite reviewed by industrial psychologists and further refined by other experts, and ultimately produced a model of the principalship that divides it into four major themes (organizational, programmatic, interpersonal, and contextual) and twenty-one separate performance domains. States have followed suit. Massachusetts, for example, adopted regulations for the evaluation of administrators that identify six general "principles of effective administrative leadership," covering twenty-seven different areas reflected in ninety-two descriptors of ideal behaviors and skills.[11]

Embedded in these taxonomies, notes Thomas Sergiovanni, is the expectation that the leader be adept at applying three sources of authority:

1. *Bureaucratic*. This emphasizes formal position and official power. It relies on rules and regulations, roles and expectations. It assumes that supervisors are more expert than staff and that accountability should

be external. Sergiovanni summarizes this approach to leadership as "expect and inspect."[12]

2. *Technical.* This emphasizes logic and research and prizes technical knowledge and objective evidence over experience and personal judgment. It relies on research data to shape practice in standardized ways, and calls for careful monitoring and supervision, but it appeals to expertise. I would summarize this approach as "logic and research."

3. *Psychological.* This emphasizes cooperation and communication and rests on interpersonal skill and motivational technique. It presumes that although staff and management have different priorities, their differences can be negotiated and compromised. Management's goals will be better accomplished if staff needs are met. Sergiovanni sees the primary leadership strategy here as "expect and reward."[13]

Generally, these three sources of authority are used in conjunction with one another. Although there are periodic proposals of so-called "one-best-way" models of leadership (such as TQM), many management experts agree that no single form of leading is optimal for all settings. Rather, they suggest that different kinds of organizations require different kinds of management and, more important, that managers within a given setting need to be able to apply a range of skills as the particular context requires.

As applied to school administration, this technical approach has enhanced leaders' organizational skills and helped them create more respectful and democratic school climates. And no leader can survive without certain core techniques, both subtle and blunt. But though management-as-technique has come to be taken for granted as sound administrative practice, its flaws are significant.

Its chief problem is that treating leadership as a list of functions or skills simply doesn't match up with real life. In daily life, no one experiences her job as a list of functions or domains or herself as a list of competencies. Leadership is a matter of a whole person in a whole environment interacting in concrete ways with other whole persons in the immediacy and unpredictability of the moment.[14] Inventories and taxonomies of leadership simply fail to capture this complexity. They miss "the whole that is greater than the sum of its parts . . . the real-world, day-to-day action" of school leaders.[15] It's not that the particular functions or skills are irrelevant, but that the business of actually leading cannot be reduced to a list. In addition, the lists are endless. As the complexities of organizational life multiply, experts keep enlarging the leadership catalogue: more domains, more tasks, more techniques; more to do, more to learn. The cure has become another part of the problem because it requires yet more from the overtaxed leader.

The List of Styles Approach

The extension of the list of functions approach is the list of styles approach, or as I think of it, the Myers-Briggs Fallacy. Ever since situational leadership gained wide popularity in management theory and training in the 1990s,[16] interpersonal flexibility has been enshrined as a primary leadership virtue. The ideal leader is seen as having a rich repertoire of people skills and can thus respond effectively to a wide variety of situations and issues. The various skills themselves are usually grouped into constellations and defined as leadership styles. Advocates of situational leadership see a leader as preferring a predominant style based on his experience, education, and training—but also as flexible. He can learn to adapt his style to the requirements of different situations. This brings us to the pinnacle of the style movement and, for me, the peak of folly in the whole realm of leadership-as-technique: The Myers-Briggs.

It is hard to find a school administrator who has not attended a workshop on the Myers-Briggs Type Inventory (MBTI) or a similar "style workshop." The MBTI and its imitators have participants answer questions about themselves and score their answers on various scales, from which they then sort themselves into different types. The workshop that follows aims to help them learn more about their particular styles and those of others with whom they work, and develop ways to communicate better by modifying these styles. To most school leaders, even those who haven't attended such a workshop, "knowledge and skill about how to motivate, apply the correct leadership style, boost morale, and engineer the right interpersonal climate [are] the 'core technology' of the education administration profession."[17] Just as a good teacher should have a repertoire of instructional strategies so as to match the learning styles of each of her students, so an administrator should have a flexible inventory of leadership approaches that generate the right results from different constituents. Unfortunately, the MBTI and the larger leadership style edifice are built on a house of cards.

Despite its popularity, the MBTI has no scientific basis. Its creators, who had no psychometric credentials, based it on the theories of Carl Jung, which, to put it mildly, are not widely accepted within the field of psychology. Studies keep showing that the test fails the basic scientific requirements of reliability and validity. This is hardly surprising, because the MBTI assumes that the test takers themselves are their own best judges. The test produces a "reported type," but a so-called "best fit process" allows test takers to modify this— to choose their own type if they dislike the test results. In addition, it turns out that many people's types vary according to the time of the day they take the MBTI and that those who retake it often end up being assigned to a different type the second time.[18]

But it is perhaps the MBTI's most fundamental flaw that, ironically, may account for its popularity, a phenomenon psychologists call "the subjective validation effect," or the Forer Effect: our tendency to accept as accurate descriptions of our personalities that are so general that they could apply to many people.[19] Sixty years ago, psychologist Bertram Forer administered to university students a test he told them was a measure of personality, ignored their answers, then distributed to each student the "evaluation" that had supposedly emerged from his or her responses, and asked each to rate the evaluation's accuracy. The students were amazed at the test's precision; their average rating was 4.2 out of a possible 5. The problem? Forer had given all the students exactly the same description, one he had taken from a newspaper astrology column. Versions of this experiment have been widely repeated, with the recipients' average ratings consistently hovering around 4.2 out of 5.

The issues here, of course, are not just the weaknesses of the MBTI and other style "tests" but the larger misunderstanding and misuse of the concept of leadership style now so prevalent in school circles. It is quite true that we *have* different styles; it is entirely false to suggest we can *change* our styles. We all have our own habits, tendencies, beliefs, and values; there is no way to disguise these from those with whom we work closely over a sustained period of time.[20] This is not to say we can't profit from learning about different styles. Within limits, we can. Doing so can help us not to take personally behavior that we dislike in others; every now and then we may remind ourselves that it is just their style, not, say, deliberate disrespect. And I have seen some work groups that were suffering severe, basic dysfunctions benefit from talking about styles as an introductory, ice-breaking step on the road to conflict resolution. But style is rooted in personality. It is inborn and unchangeable. We may change *what* we think and believe but not *how* we think and believe. We may undergo a religious conversion, leaving one faith and joining another, and this may be life altering and cause a profound change in our outlook on life, but we will be the same *kind* of believer in the second denomination that we were in the first.

Even if it were possible to change styles, this would only complicate and weaken leadership. It would give the leader yet more to do. Trying to master the style catalogue is itself an additional burden, one that fosters the stress-inducing expectation that a good leader can—and should—be all things to all people, regularly adapting his behavior to meet the styles of others. This reduces him to following everyone else. Moreover, responding to a wide range of situations in a variety of different ways necessarily makes a leader seem inconsistent and thus harder to follow. Even worse, leaders who base their practice on styles frequently come across not just as inconsistent but as insincere and artificial, as studied and calculated, rather than spontaneous and genuine.[21] No leadership style seminar turns an anxious, controlling principal who cannot delegate tasks into a confident, trusting principal who shares responsibility. At best, it may help turn him into an anxious, controlling principal who is *trying to act* confident and trusting. But he won't be inspiring confidence or trust. Imagine that you are having a lively discussion with your boss about an important issue when it suddenly dawns on you that he is applying a technique to you. If you are like most people, your instant response is to draw back; a gap has suddenly arisen between you. His words now take on a different meaning. Leadership that is *based on* techniques and styles is actually not leadership. It is manipulation, and it is ultimately self-defeating.

Learning and Leading from Strength

None of this denies the importance of leaders' learning, changing, growing, and applying skills. It's not as if savvy principals, school heads, and superintendents refuse to read books or attend conferences or try new approaches. They do all of these things. But as I noted at the outset, they generally don't go looking for gurus and wizards. And when they do seek advice, they don't lose their bearings; they adapt what they adopt.

One plot summary of *The Wizard of Oz* describes the Wizard as solving the problems of Dorothy and her companions "through common sense and a little double talk . . . suggesting that, in fact, they had what they were searching for all along."[22] Now and then, common sense and a little double talk are probably helpful in leading any organization. But what really makes leaders savvy is knowing what they have—that is, knowing themselves. They use new inputs to adjust their own approaches but they unapologetically modify these new methods to "fit who I am," as one superintendent says. They learn—and lead—from strength.

We will explore this concept in depth in Chapter Five. For now, we can note that contrary to conventional wisdom, the leaders of high-performing organizations are not would-be "stylemasters." Rather, they tend to be people of strong character with strong commitments who maximize their strengths. Responsible organizational experts keep pointing out that when we look at successful organizations we find a wide range of styles among their leaders. Peter Vaill has captured this vividly: "There are tyrants whose almost maniacal commitment to achieving the system's purposes makes one think that they'd be locked up. . . . There are warm, laid-back parent figures who hardly seem to be doing anything at all, until one looks a little more closely. There are technocrats . . . and dreamers. . . . Some are rah-rah optimists and others are dour critics who express their love for the system by enumerating its imperfections."[23]

It was fifteen years ago that I first read Vaill's summary, but I still recall the impact it had on me. Though he was describing corporate settings, I realized immediately that the same thing was true in the schools where I worked. It has remained true in the years since. The leaders of top districts and schools are by no means all similar: some are intensely hands-on, others are great delegators; some don't hesitate to criticize poor performance, others accentuate the positive; some care mostly about basic skills, others about higher-order ones. What they share in common is self-knowledge and commitment. Not long after I read Vaill's description I gathered a group of principals from high-achieving schools to discuss their different approaches to leadership. As we were finishing up, one of them said simply, "We're obviously different, but we each know ourselves and we each know what we're about."

Savvy leaders illustrate a truth with tremendous liberating potential, one we will explore in later chapters: there are many ways to lead successfully. They know that the key is not to chase some ideal—a composite list of virtues from the management bookshelf—but to be the very best of who they are.

Chapter Two

THE SECOND SECRET

They'll Never Understand

Some things in life can never be fully appreciated or understood by a virgin.

—Burton Malkiel[1]

L EADERS WHO LAST LEARN TO BITE THEIR TONGUES. THERE IS a long list of things they dare not ask in public. Two at the top of this list are "Why don't they see?" and "What about me?" Dozens of times a year a school leader somewhere asks me some version of both, hoping there is a way to get faculty or parents or other constituents to grasp the full context of a decision, a dilemma, or a process and to be less disapproving, if not actually appreciative.

Sometimes their focus is external, involving politics ("How do we make our parents see that this is no time to ask the city for a big budget increase?") or legalities ("How do we get people to accept that special ed is a legal entitlement, one that we can't just cut despite its cost?"). More often their focus is internal, involving personnel ("Faculty act like I'm a sadist for not renewing a teacher they know is flat-out incompetent") or power ("They accuse me of not listening to them; I do listen and I do understand their views, I just disagree") or procedure ("They say they want their 'voices' to be heard, but they never come to meetings").

Often the leaders feel damned if they do and damned if they don't ("They said I was never in classrooms, so I made it a priority and now they say I'm spying on them") or mistreated ("I've been interviewing candidates nonstop and writing evaluations nonstop and all the teachers do is complain that I'm invisible"). Not infrequently, they're just plain fed up ("The whining is getting to me. I feel like saying, 'Grow up! Stop complaining and do your job!'").

Almost always, the root of these questions and concerns is a wish that others would *understand*. Understand that many complexities factor into a decision, accept that not everything can be explained in public, appreciate the burdens of being everybody's go-to person, trust the leader's expertise and good will, take a broad perspective on the school as a whole and its long-term interests. Just *understand*. They won't. This is a vain hope. They'll never understand, not fully. In leading, as in so much of life, there is simply no substitute for actual experience; those who haven't done it can't truly know what it is like.

A savvy leader knows this. A savvy leader knows that, in the first place, it's not fair to expect others to understand, to view things from a position they have never occupied. Perspective, after all, is everything. People who've never taught can't appreciate what it's like to face a class, whether of first graders or twelfth graders. People who've never led a school or a district can't appreciate its burdens. Where you stand, as the old saying goes, depends on where you sit. But the main reason that the hope is vain is that the issues above are inevitable. They are never local phenomena, or never just local phenomena. A savvy leader knows that they are built into the nature of leadership, into the very essence of organizational life and human relationships. Indeed, what they illustrate is a set of five underlying dilemmas that are inherent in leading almost any organization and certainly any educational institution.

Before looking at these dilemmas, I want to draw a vital distinction: they are not problems. This difference is one I learned from Matthew King, a savvy leader of both public and independent schools. A problem, Matt says, has a solution; you fix it. A dilemma is built into life; you cope with it. I think of the difference this way. A problem is when the muffler on your car is dragging; you have it replaced. It's fixed. A dilemma is being a parent. Your children are yours, but you must let them go; you love them but you could kill them; they make you feel proud and fulfilled but terrified and furious; it's wonderful being with them but fabulous to get away from them. There is no cure for any of this. No book or expert can fix it. You're not helpless; you respond, you manage, you make progress, you *cope*. But you don't just resolve a dilemma once and for all. It recurs periodically in different forms and must be addressed each time, often in different ways.

The difference between problems and dilemmas is about expectations. When we see something as a problem, we expect to solve it. If our solution doesn't last, we assume we've erred. When we see something as a dilemma, we know we must do our best but we don't expect to overcome it permanently. None of the five natural tensions in leadership below are problems. None is fixable in any permanent way. Savvy leaders accept this. They adapt their approaches and expectations accordingly and learn to maximize their leverage where they can.

Managing Versus Leading

In future chapters, I will use "management" and "leadership" in roughly interchangeable ways. This is routine in the organizational literature, but some observers have distinguished the two, most notably Warren Bennis and Bert Nanus, who famously said that managers do things right but leaders do the right thing.[2] In this view, leading is the exercise of high-level conceptual skills and decisiveness. It is envisioning mission, developing strategy, inspiring personnel, and transforming culture. Managing, however, is mundane. It is making sure purchase orders are completed, policies promulgated, procedures followed.

Clearly, conceiving new ways to promote professional discourse among teachers is not only a higher-order task than, say, suppressing students' vandalism of bathrooms, it is also more rewarding. Unfortunately, as all of us who have ever led anything know, you spend most of your day enmeshed in management. You step out of your office and someone asks, "Have you got a minute?" What do you say? Do you say, "Yes, I do. Indeed I do. I've been sitting on my ass all morning and it's really boring in here. I'm so glad you caught me and I am fully at your disposal. How can I help?"

It's not just the interruptions. Running any organization, especially a school, seems to be a matter of solving an endless set of messes.[3] Most school leaders, like most executives elsewhere, have always spent far more time managing messes than, say, transforming culture. In fact, efforts to exert leadership are usually cut short by the need to manage these messes. Studies have long shown that executives of all types tend to work "at an unrelenting pace," with their activities notable for their "brevity, variety, and discontinuity."[4] Long episodes of high-level conceptualization and reflection are rare. I remember fondly the principal who told me that his job was "more high dreck than high tech. It's day after day of 'Guess what just happened.'" When Warren Bennis decided to apply his expertise in leadership by becoming a college president, he quickly learned two lessons: "routine work drives out nonroutine work and smothers to death all creative planning, all fundamental change," and "make whatever grand plans you will, you may be sure the unexpected or the trivial will disturb and disrupt them."[5]

During three decades of consulting with school leaders I've not only been told about hundreds of intrusions by the unexpected and trivial, I've experienced them personally. Years ago I described a visit to a high school principal I'll call Tom Black. Tom was disenchanted with his school's heavy emphasis on separate academic disciplines and teacher-centered lecturing. As he sought to promote interdisciplinary courses and a new orientation toward teaching and learning, he encountered significant faculty resistance. One morning we sat down to discuss these issues. Tom was elaborating his philosophy of student-centered teaching and his plan to engage the faculty in a reconsideration of the school's mission and values when we were interrupted by a call from the Department of Public Works. A major water main had broken and the school would have no water for the rest of the day—no water to prepare lunch or flush toilets.

Tom called his superintendent to ask if the school should be closed. After a few minutes of discussion there was a long pause, and then Tom asked, "And you think teenagers won't take advantage of that?" The response must have been something like, "I know you'll do your best." Tom made noises of reluctant agreement. The superintendent had decided that students could not be sent home—few parents would be at home to receive them—and that those who needed to use the bathroom would be transported by bus to a nearby elementary school. Tom had to announce the water cutoff over the public address system and advise all students needing to use the bathroom to report to the office for busing. We terminated our leadership discussion so he could go manage.

It's not just the unexpected interruptions, of course. There is also the sheer social complexity of organizational life itself. The fulfillment of official job descriptions is affected by such things as politics—power struggles between different interest groups, conflicts over resources and status, and so on. But a key part of this complexity is what one middle school principal wryly called "the annoying reality that people have personal lives." To achieve the goals her district has set for her school, she calculated that she would need her faculty to be "almost perpetually available; fully engaged at school twelve hours a day; never out sick; and planning, collaborating, and grading much of the weekend." She was reflecting on the fact that in her school, as in most, there has been a demographic shift. Many of her teachers are relatively young, having recently replaced the older generation that had long predominated and has now retired. Her school now has a steady stream of maternity leaves and a rising number of days that teachers miss school to take care of their own children who fall ill. "Their problem," the principal says, "is that teaching here is not compatible with being a parent, or having a family—or having a life. Mine is how much time I spend finding substitutes, supporting and comforting them— and cleaning up the messes they cause."

Resources Versus Demands

I have rarely met a leader in any organization who felt that the resources available were adequate to meet the demands of the job. I have found a sense of insufficiency ubiquitous among leaders of both private corporations and public agencies and, within each of these sectors, among leaders of both comparatively poor institutions and comparatively wealthy ones. Leaders perpetually feel caught between, on the one hand, the realities of limited supply and, on the other, the requests of clients for more services and of staff for more resources. "Resources" usually comes down to "money," either directly or indirectly (more staff, more materials). But no matter how much money is available, it rarely seems to be enough. Nor, it seems, are there ever enough people (or enough good people) or enough time or enough materials or enough space.

This sense of scarcity is probably rooted in human nature. We cannot live for long in any system (a family, a workplace) without coming to take for granted certain regularities, patterns, and traditions. Over time, as external demands grow or change, they can put pressure on these taken-for-granteds, but we find it increasingly difficult to imagine responding except in the ways we have come to depend on. In my experience, this is a key reason why it is so much more common that a new chief executive hired from outside—who doesn't share the internal culture and mind-set—is able and willing to cut staff, slash overhead, redefine roles, rearrange work groups, and so on.

In American education, the imbalance between resources and demands has always been endemic, dating back to the days of one-room schoolhouses and teacher compensation that amounted to bare subsistence. This imbalance plays itself out in two ways. At the most immediate level, there are vast disparities between wealthy schools and poor ones, disparities that have never been greater. The resources typically available to educate our neediest students are grossly inadequate and dwarfed by those available to educate our most advantaged. Generations of leaders in many of our high-poverty schools and districts have never known anything but scarcity: they have too many teachers who are inexperienced, poorly trained, and uncertified; too few textbooks and too many that are outdated; not enough computers; large class sizes; and, often, buildings that are in bad repair and marked by violence. Many of their students are especially challenging to teach and need much more time and attention than the school can make available. Over time, this combination of low support and high need fosters hopelessness and apathy—so much to do, so few resources—which then reduce students' prospects even further.

The contrast between conditions in these schools and those in America's richest couldn't be more unfair. But in my experience they do not mean that most wealthier schools have adequate resources to accomplish what is expected of them either. On the contrary, deprivation is always relative— not to other schools but to the demands upon one's own school. Typically, parents who are providing higher levels of funding expect higher returns on their investment. In the nation's premier school districts and independent schools the predominant sense is not one of elegant sufficiency but of recurrent anxiety about accelerating expectations and entitled consumerism among parents, growing numbers of whom see their tax (or tuition) dollars as purchasing a service—indeed, an outcome—for which the school itself is responsible. Moreover, in schools that serve wealthy families and enjoy good facilities, small class sizes, and so on, faculty often find it hard to believe (and leaders are often reluctant to announce) that some key decisions are caused by financial constraints. Though the imbalance between resources and demands is a challenge for leaders in most organizations, it is deeply, profoundly embedded in schools everywhere.

The Paradox of Power: The Dependent Leader

As with resources, so with power: leaders rarely feel they have enough. In most organizations few people admit to having *any* real power: everyone feels fettered, either by internal forces or external constraints.[6] Most of us tend to imagine that if we could move up in the hierarchy we would acquire *real* power and then could truly effect change. Educators who seek careers in administration often do so with this in mind. They become principals in part to "make a difference," to right wrongs and correct flaws that chafed them as teachers and to assert a vision of schooling as it should be. The first great shock awaiting them is discovering how little power they truly have.

When a teacher ascends to the principalship he immediately begins to realize how much he depends on his former colleagues. He can exert sway over the character and climate of a school and eventually the thrust of its teaching, but day in and day out the staff are the ones who must actually translate his goals into action and who, enjoying the protections of union, tenure, and tradition (academic freedom), generally have wide latitude to implement—or not—his priorities. School administrators, even those in independent schools whose teachers are not unionized, have much less control over their staffs than most corporate executives enjoy. Indeed, independent schools are not only independent as institutions, they are full of independent people—teachers who prize their autonomy and often resist initiatives that encroach on their freedom to teach as they wish. A similar dynamic is part of the culture of many high-performing suburban public schools. These limits on the leader's power constitute just one of many reasons why corporate models of leadership rarely fit schools well.

Some principals try again, moving up to become central office administrators and superintendents. But the higher a person rises, the less direct contact she has with the organization's staff and clients, the more attenuated and filtered her personal influence becomes—and the more subject to misinterpretation are her actions. Of course, in any direct encounter a superior is more powerful than a subordinate, but the experience of leading, especially when it comes to getting large numbers of people to change, often leaves leaders far more aware of their vulnerability than of their power. Tom Black recalled vividly his first announcement to the faculty of the changes he wanted them to make. "Standing there in front of them, knowing how much they would dislike my plan and how impossible it would be for me to convince them all and stay on top of them, I felt anything but powerful."

This vulnerability is reflected in the difficulty of balancing substance and symbolism. People who seek leadership positions so that they can make a difference expect to be engaged in substantive matters of policy and purpose, only to discover that they become hostages to ritual. Here again, the higher the position, the further removed it is from hands-on activity and the more its occupant is confined to gestures that are primarily symbolic. At the highest levels of public office one spends vast amounts of time in such gestures. It's not just that symbolism is draining—a steady diet of "showing the flag," "pressing the flesh," and "sending signals" wears on one—but that it often ends up being so much more important to a leader's success than substance. One superintendent, reflecting back on his first year in the role, remembered that from September through Thanksgiving he spent every weekend working on an improved curriculum development process for the district. "I was fully engaged in furthering our core educational purpose," he said, "but I wasn't at any Saturday football games. The school board raked me over the coals for not being visible and not fostering school spirit." The pressure to concentrate on creating perceptions is both intense and, for many leaders, debilitating.

The Parental Transference Object

Leaders everywhere are fond of referring to their unit as a "family." The metaphor is ubiquitous in all sorts of organizations, including the largest corporations and the most cutthroat. But even in these settings, which in size and context are most unfamilial, there is one family factor that is almost always present: the leader becomes a parental transference object.

Transference was Freud's term to describe what happens when we project our perceptions and expectations of person A onto person B and then interact with B as though he or she were A. The roots of this projection usually lie in our childhood relationship with a parent. "Parental transference object" is psychological shorthand for the fact that we are all inclined to react to an authority figure much as we did to a parent. This dynamic is readily visible in our reactions to political leaders. We mock and ridicule politicians, but we all long to be led—not bossed, but led. We want someone we can look up to, trust, and follow. We make all sorts of positive assumptions about candidates we find appealing and all sorts of negative assumptions about those we don't.

If you doubt the power of this kind of parental projection onto a leader, I invite you to imagine this scenario. You're a principal away from school on a Friday attending a professional conference. During a break you telephone your school and, choosing a teacher at random, leave this message: "Hi, John. As you know, I'm away today, but I've been thinking about you. I'll be back on Monday. Would you stop in and see me? Thanks." And you hang up.

John will not have a good weekend. He's likely to spend it imagining the worst, or at least worrying that he has somehow displeased you. But if your superintendent called you from a conference she was attending and left you a similar message, you wouldn't have a good weekend, either. You, too, would probably imagine the worst or at least worry that you had displeased her in some way. And if the school board president telephoned her and left such a message, she would not have a good weekend, either, and would probably spend it in much the same way.

None of this has to do with intelligence or the logical, but with emotions and the psychological. The roots of transference are deep, primitive, and nonrational. The leader can't resolve the matter by explaining to John, "You're responding to me as though I were your father, who was apparently critical and disapproving. I'm not him. Please stop reacting this way."

I don't want to exaggerate the transference dynamic. It doesn't usually dictate the relationship between leader and staff. Many leaders enjoy strong, positive connections with their people, connections that are both professional and personal, congenial and collegial, and that foster rational discussion and decision making. But at some level for everyone, and particularly for some people, parental transference can be an important influence. When an aspect—even a small one—of an issue or a decision touches something meaningful to us, transference can loom large. And when it does, the leader cannot escape it.

Isolation in a Fishbowl

Closely related to the parental transference phenomenon is the paradox of being at once isolated and exposed. All the old jokes about it being lonely at the top are rooted in truth; leading is lonely work. Leaders' roles are notable for their isolation (a principal or head literally has no peer in the school, nor does a superintendent in the district). Moreover, they must frequently assume parental roles as monitors, policymakers, bearers of bad news, and rule enforcers. The most sustained, if not the most dramatic, change in moving from a staff position into a leadership role is the loss of peers. A teacher who is promoted to principal may continue to enjoy trusting and rewarding relationships with faculty, but is inevitably distanced from them. Becoming a leader enlarges his responsibility. His focus must now be the whole staff, indeed the whole school, not just his classroom or department. Promotion also diminishes support. If a tornado rips the roof off the building, if a teacher dies of a sudden heart attack, if parents are concerned about a controversial curriculum topic, it is the principal who will be called and who will have to respond. He will not always have to respond entirely alone, but he will usually have to respond first and orchestrate the responses of others, who will take their cues from him. And many key leadership decisions, especially sensitive ones, are made in relative isolation.

The hardest of these are the ones that must be made in private but that have very public consequences, situations in which it is either impolitic or illegal to explain openly the full context of the decision. Toughest of all, most school leaders agree, are decisions to let a teacher go. Here is a common scenario. The head of school has bent over backward to give an underperforming teacher time and help to improve and, having finally concluded that the situation is hopeless, terminates the teacher and offers a severance package, whereupon the teacher begins to complain bitterly to colleagues (and sometimes parents and students) about the gross injustice he is suffering. The head must suffer in silence. She cannot call a faculty meeting to detail the teacher's shortcomings ("As you know, Fred has been a mediocre teacher at best. The school has given him three years of coaching but he seems immune to improvement. His departure will mean addition by subtraction. Moreover, we are giving him a half-year's salary"). Fred's colleagues will be up in arms. After Fred is gone, many will acknowledge that his departure was appropriate. But the head will still bear the scars from the process.

And it is not just the leader's decisions that are public but the leader as well. A principal or superintendent is constantly in the public eye throughout the school community. Like clergy, school leaders are always seen as "in role." When Robert Spillane was superintendent of the Fairfax, Virginia, schools, he said his job made him "a celebrity of sorts. People know who you are, and they see your picture on television. . . . But the loneliness is that you're always 'on,' you're always performing as superintendent."[7] Of the many ironies in school leadership, this is one of the sharpest: to be so alone in public. It is, I'm convinced, one of the reasons administrators attend (and, as Chapter Seven urges, *should* attend) so many conferences. Under the guise of pursuing professional development they get to mingle freely with their peers, who are similarly imprisoned—and who *understand*.

Danger and Opportunity

These dilemmas are not new in nature—chiefs have always had to contend with them—but what is new is their extent and intensity. The changing nature of organizational life has exacerbated them to the point of disempowering leaders and diminishing the quality of their lives. With a few exceptions, virtually every sector of American public life, from heavy industry and financial services to the media, medicine, and law, has undergone dramatic change in its basic assumptions and practices and now operates in an ever more complex and vulnerable context. This is abundantly true in education.

For more than twenty years there have been calls on all sides for inspired, transformational leadership of our schools. But the opportunities for such lofty activity have shrunk, while the management burdens of actually running a school have mushroomed. This is due in good part to the relentless growth of regulatory demands and restrictions. A sharp rise in the number of students with significant disabilities coupled with chronic underfunding of special education (SPED) would have been problematic enough (a classic resources-versus-demands dilemma that has intensified), but they have been accompanied by a vast expansion of parents' legal rights and ever more specific requirements for testing and treating students. SPED regulations (and the mind-numbing paper-work they require) have become a chronic headache for schools. So, too, have the procedures for administering the tests mandated by No Child Left Behind, the provisions for building security (including lock-down drills), even the legal-ities of dealing with students' allergies or sending students on field trips. All of these have multiplied management chal-lenges and reduced the orbit for leading.

Also more pronounced is the public loneliness of leaders. Difficult decisions that distress people and that cannot be fully explained risk much more intense and sustained public reaction these days. Parents, who, as noted, increasingly see themselves as customers, are more likely to go public with their disappointment, anger, or criticism, sharing their views with other parents during the carpool pickup or via e-mail. And though not yet the norm, it is now much more common for a disgruntled teacher who is not being rehired to go public, sending lengthy e-mails attacking the principal to colleagues and to parents, sometimes even the press. Speaking of the press, school leaders everywhere, in large cities and small towns, complain that the reporters and editors are now much less well informed about education, much more eager to take literally complaints about schools and to dramatize even relatively small issues that come to their attention.

No wonder, then, that savvy leaders acquire such a healthy skepticism. In the coming chapters we will examine some of the factors in the current context of schooling that contribute to this skepticism by exacerbating the built-in dilemmas of leadership, including the extraordinary, unrealistic increases in our expectations of schools and hence of their leaders, and the family and social changes that are complicating their efforts to fulfill their responsibilities. For now, we can note that savvy leaders do not just endure these tensions, they respect them. They do not automatically see them as reflecting unique flaws in themselves or in others in their school community. Of course, there are always characteristics unique to every issue in a school, but savvy leaders remind themselves that often the *kind* of issue comes with the territory. This is not a reason to minimize it, but it is a reason not to magnify it—and not to take it personally, a natural tendency that makes coping more difficult.

A savvy leader also knows that these tensions bring not only danger but opportunity. The opportunities may be smaller and less frequent than the dangers, but are therefore all the more crucial. Thus, although it is true that leadership is a higher-order activity than management and hence seems more important, it is equally true that no organization, least of all a school, can succeed if it is not well managed. Leaders who are charismatic and visionary but who are disorganized, who can't structure plans and meetings, sow confusion and frustration among their people. A smart superintendent or principal envisions *and* organizes. If he can only envision, he hires and empowers assistants who organize.

Similarly, although being a parental transference object and having one's days enmeshed in symbolism can be draining, they are also sources of influence, making it easier to be heard and respected—and followed—when communicating messages and implementing priorities. Effective leaders are good parents and symbolists. Like both, they communicate most forcefully by what they do, not just what they say. Norman Colb, who has experienced remarkable success both as a superintendent and an independent school head, likens leading a school to being a radio beacon. "Whether consciously or not," he says, "the leader's actions send powerful messages, which, over time, shape the school community to its core." This is one reason Norm has chosen to do lunch duty, making it a point to talk with as many students as possible each day. He began doing so "simply because I wanted the fun of interacting with them, but I soon learned that the faculty was watching and that what they saw was that in this school, spending time with students is a pleasure, not a burden."[8]

Not infrequently, the parental and symbolic dimensions of the role mean that a school leader ends up serving as a kind of priest in a secular parish, hearing confessions, offering blessings, assigning penances. The opportunities for exercising these roles often occur unexpectedly: granting extra leave to a teacher who has a family medical emergency, counseling parents who are getting divorced and worried about the impact on their children. The terrorist attacks of September 11, 2001, as awful as they were, provided a powerful example of the parental and symbolic power of school leaders. In the days that followed, principals and heads all over America rediscovered how much they mattered. Simply by being visible, by appearing at the front of the school in the morning to greet students and parents, by walking the corridors, by sending letters home, they served as reassuring figures, symbols of continuity and predictability during a time of traumatic uncertainty. "I've never made more of an impact than I did that week, and it was essentially by just being my role," a principal said. "As soon as I realized this, I dropped everything else and became 'The Visible Principal.'"

Moments like these confirm the importance and power of leadership. They confirm, too, that the essence of good leadership is simple—not, as I've already noted and will note again, easy, but simple—and therefore readily overlooked. But savvy leaders don't overlook the simple essentials. They are realists who've learned to moderate their expectations— they know people won't understand—and so they've become opportunists who seize their moments. And as we shall see in the next chapter, when we turn to the challenge of leading change, and then in future chapters, when we enlarge our perspective to examine the broader context within which leaders and their schools function, the need to combine moderation and opportunism has never been more pressing.

Chapter Three

The Third Secret

Change Is What It Means

To make dreams apparent to others and to align people with them [requires not just] mere explanation or clarification but the creation of meaning.

—Warren Bennis[1]

IN EDUCATION, AS IN MOST SPHERES OF AMERICAN PUBLIC LIFE, leadership and change have become inseparable. The conventional wisdom has long been that most of our schools are failing and that even the best are not preparing students adequately for the world of the future. Innovation is therefore seen as both a necessity and an opportunity, its pursuit as leadership's defining purpose. This emphasis has led to, and been fostered by, real growth in the knowledge base about leading change. For all the quackery and quick fixes in the popular management literature, there have been some terrific contributions, both within the field of education by, among others, Michael Fullan, Lee Bolman and Terrence Deal, Andy Hargreaves, Philip Schlechty, and Thomas Sergiovanni, and within the field of organization development by, among others, Edgar Schein, the grand master of organizational culture, Warren Bennis, James Kouzes and Barry Posner, and Peter Vaill, as well as by writers in other fields, most notably Peter Marris, who brilliantly captured the key connection between change and loss.

Unfortunately, even though these and other top-notch thinkers have written many books, and those in the first group have appeared widely at educational conferences over many years, their insights remain vastly underapplied in the actual practice of school leadership in America. Indeed, the demand for rapid improvement has promoted approaches to change that contradict their wisdom, treating the school as a factory or a service company and the leader as a corporate turnaround specialist whose success is to be measured by a simplistic bottom line (students' test scores). This primitive approach may be relevant in industrial and corporate workplaces, but it ignores the unique features of schools and the special challenges of leading innovation there.

Like the sharpest school thinkers, the sharpest school leaders do not make this error. They know that change naturally provokes ambivalence and resistance, that this is particularly true in schools, and that whether faculty embrace innovation depends not on whether outsiders think they need to but on their own readiness to do so. Key to creating this readiness is shaping the meaning of the change. Savvy leaders do this through a combination of pressure and support.

Understanding Resistance

America is a nation founded in revolution, peopled by immigrants and seekers of new frontiers, fueled by a sense of its own exceptionalism and a deep-seated belief in the potential for individual and collective progress. This outlook has culminated, as Chapter One noted, in a worship of innovation and of the faster, more productive life. The belief that we must prepare ourselves and our children for even greater rates of change is widely and firmly established. Hence the emphasis on creating "learning organizations" capable of continuous improvement. The cutting edge is the place to be.

In real life things are not nearly so simple. Change almost always causes ambivalence and resistance. We know that change is inevitable. We know Heraclitus's maxim that "no man ever steps in the same river twice, for it's not the same river and he's not the same man." We often hope for change, for our own lives and relationships and careers to be different. Yet at the core we remain conservative creatures, our psychology marked by a powerful preference for predictability. We routinely resist change when it occurs, especially when imposed on us by others. This conservatism is not political but a deep impulse to preserve continuity and familiarity in life. In his wonderful book, *Loss and Change*, Peter Marris makes a compelling case that life depends on continuity and that in virtually every significant transition of any kind, acceptance and adjustment prove far more difficult than anticipated for all concerned. This has certainly been my experience in the schools and organizations where I have consulted, in the clinic I direct, in the individuals and families I have treated, and in my own life. Whether a change is planned or unplanned, personal or professional, large or small, welcome or unwelcome; whether we take the perspective of reformers or their targets, of people or organizations, the nearly universal result is ambivalence.[2]

This is because human beings are, as the late Harvard paleontologist Stephen Jay Gould said, "pattern-seeking animals."[3] Pattern seeking is actually hardwired into our brains, visible even in the behavior of newborn infants, and vital to our very existence: our ability to make sense of events—and to adjust to new circumstances—depends crucially on continuity, on the validity of what we have learned and how we have learned it.[4] So, too, does our ability to find meaning in life. Our lives cannot be meaningful unless we can construct and preserve a coherent, predictable pattern in events and relationships. *Meaning* here has two main components: *understanding* ("I see what you mean") and *attachment to people and ideas* ("you mean so much to me"; "teaching a child to read means so much to me"). How we react to any change depends above all on what it means to us, that is, how it affects the understandings and attachments by which we live. The impact of any particular innovation always hinges on many factors, including, among others, our individual characteristics (personality, history), the kind of organization we work in, the nature of the change, the way it is presented to us, and so on. But at best, our reaction is likely to be mixed. For though the public meanings of change, as it is typically promoted, are cast in terms of growth and development, progress and renewal, and though these can often be the ultimate result of change, its private meanings are about resistance, not acceptance: they start with loss and include, among others, incompetence and conflict.

Growth and *development* may be the ideal synonyms for change, but *grief* and *bereavement* are every bit as accurate. We are bereaved when someone we love dies, but we are also bereaved when an assumption we take for granted is devalued. This kind of grief is not usually as intense as that caused by the death of a loved one (though it can be), but it provokes a similar mourning often marked by disbelief, denial, sadness, and anger. The pattern each of us constructs that makes our lives meaningful is formed in a context of specific relationships and circumstances and rooted in feelings and experiences that have great emotional significance. It can rarely be altered just by rational explanation. We can't just discard familiar understandings and powerful attachments in the name of an "impersonal utilitarian calculation of the common good."[5] In this regard, change agents often overlook a crucial fact: patterns create meaning through continuity, not happiness. We become attached not just to positive patterns but to negative ones. We are often reluctant to abandon patterns even when we dislike them. We can accept—even cling to—the hopelessness of our situations. Indeed, we can become fiercely resistant to changes that promise to address the very circumstances that most distress us. When trying to understand reactions to change it is never just the logical that matters, but the psychological.[6]

A second powerful meaning of change is to threaten competence. A school promotes innovation (a new curriculum or teaching method) to enhance teachers' competence, to improve their ability to fulfill the school's mission, but the innovation typically begins by threatening their *existing* competence: it requires them to abandon something they know how to do and adopt something they don't know how to do. Alterations in practices, procedures, and routines make all of us feel inadequate and insecure, especially if we have exercised our skills in a particular way for a long time (and even more if we have seen our performance as exemplary). Ultimately, if we see the project through, we may develop new skills and knowledge and the change may come to mean progress. But this is rarely true at the outset.

Change also means conflict. Although planned innovations are usually sold as being better for everyone in the school, this is almost never true. Every major change creates winners and losers, at least at first. For example, staff often see change as imposed by administrators for their own purposes without regard to the difficulties of implementing it. Within the faculty, some people's beliefs and commitments will be better aligned with the new priorities, some people's skills and temperaments will be more relevant, some people's roles and statuses may rise faster. And old wounds may be reopened. Every staff family contains within it a history of disputes and disagreements, personal hurts, jealousies, and betrayals. Change can reawaken the memories of these events, increasing tension, diminishing cooperation, and sparking disagreements that seem to be about the change at hand but are actually about old hurts.

These three meanings of change cause resistance in all sorts of workplaces, but they certainly loom large in schools. To begin with, education is fundamentally a backward-looking, conservator's enterprise. In a nation obsessed with innovation, this may seem a condemnation; it is not. A school's function is to prepare children for the future, but it can only do this by teaching them about the past—not just history but the assembled body of knowledge in each subject and the society's key values and norms. We can only teach what we know. Moreover, much (though not all) of a school's curriculum is, if not timeless, slow changing (fractions, the periodic table, the meanings of *Hamlet*, the causes of the American Revolution, and so on) and many schools pride themselves on their devotion to enduring truths and established traditions. Good teaching is always creative, but it is not perpetually innovative; it benefits from regular refreshers and occasional overhauls, but it doesn't demand the kind of continuous updating that, say, law or medicine or high technology do. Continuity is a powerful fact of school life, just as it is in family life and religious life.

Not surprisingly, teaching attracts people for whom continuity is a good fit, people with a strong security orientation and a strong service ethic, not entrepreneurs with a thirst for risk and competition. It is the only field that offers tenure, and it draws those who, among other things, are willing to trade salary for stability. Teachers have traditionally tended to change employers much less frequently than corporate professionals, to look for a school that is a good home and to stay there. They typically thrive in—and usually prefer—the company of children and adolescents (would we want our youth taught by people who didn't?) and they try to emphasize the positive. They wish to help, nurture, foster, inspire, encourage, and bring out the best in students. They generally like people and want to be liked. They take their work very personally. All of these characteristics are good for raising the young; none of them makes it easier to manage the loss, the threat to competence, and the potential for conflict caused by change.

One cannot hope to implement change without persuading people that it is necessary. This is a task of daunting proportions that must often start by challenging people's views of themselves and their performance. Easily the most thoughtful, realistic approach that I have encountered is Edgar Schein's concept of change as "unfreezing,"[7] which he adapted from the work of the social psychologist Kurt Lewin. This approach begins by recognizing the tendency of people and systems to maintain a homeostasis. Because innovation requires the learning of something new and, usually, the unlearning of something old, it causes anxiety. As we have seen, people naturally cling to their current skills and are afraid to try new ones, especially when the changes involved are large and complex or when the time frame for mastery is short or when the tolerance for error is low—all conditions that have applied in schools for several decades now. In such a context, it becomes easy to rationalize the value of the tried and true and the impracticality or impossibility of the new. As Schein presents it, unfreezing is a matter of creating a readiness to change by mobilizing one kind of anxiety, the fear of *not* trying, and by lessening another, the fear of trying. The first requires the leader to apply pressure, the second to offer support.

Pressure: Why, What, How

If people are to accept—let alone embrace—a change, they must understand its *why*, *what*, and *how*: why they can't simply preserve the status quo and keep doing what they've been doing, what they must start doing, and how they can accomplish this goal. Unless something increases the cost of preserving the status quo, unless people are sufficiently dissatisfied with the present state of affairs—and their role in maintaining it—they have no reason to endure the losses and challenges of change. Pressure can be defined as anything that makes it harder to continue the old. It ranges all the way from simply asking people, "Why do you do it that way?" to threatening to fire them if they keep doing so. Inevitably, it involves the assertion of power. Despite a strong bias against top-down leadership that remains prevalent in education, virtually every instance of successful school innovation that I've ever known of involves a powerful, adroit leader. I've never met a successful change agent who simply waited for everyone to get over their grief. Waiting for buy-in to occur spontaneously is almost always a losing strategy. Buy-in must be built and the building begins with the leader's making the case for change.

To make the case, a leader must disconfirm people's readings of their situation and their satisfaction with their present practices. This does not mean castigating and blaming them, but it often means challenging them to face realities they have preferred to avoid. Effective implementation thus begins with candid discussion. Leaders have to justify the changes they propose. This requires a clear statement outlining the current challenges and issues and the risks of continuing with the current ways of coping (*why*), the old practices that must be abandoned and the new ones to be adopted (*what*), and the concrete help that will support the implementation (*how*). Simple. But not easy.

Many school leaders are good at the *what* and the *how*, but give short shrift to the *why*, which is the most important. Explaining why the status quo can't continue is usually where the loss begins—and where negative feelings are engendered—but it cannot be avoided. Without it, there is no readiness, no motivation to change. Without readiness and motivation, even top-notch training is ineffective. To the surprise of many leaders, presenting the *why* can be unexpectedly difficult in schools that see themselves as successful. If students have typically performed well; if the school has historically been sought after; if placement of students into the next level (secondary school, college) has generally been good; and if there has been a strong tradition of teacher autonomy, faculty often feel, "It ain't broke; don't fix it." But in any school, presenting the *why* can cause distress. It confronts a school with its shortcomings, with the gaps between teachers' professed goals and students' actual outcomes. It usually involves raising people's guilt by noting how their performance violates a shared ideal ("We say we believe that every child can learn, but the gap between our best and worst performers is widening") or raising their anxiety by noting how their performance threatens their well-being ("We asked for new staffing to improve literacy, but our results are no better; if they don't improve we will lose the staff, and return to our old class sizes").

One key to building buy-in is making change inevitable. The more certain a change seems, the more people are inclined to adjust to it. And when the ultimate aim is a change in beliefs and assumptions, which cannot be imposed, one must often insist on a change in behavior, which can. A key reason for this is that changes in behavior don't just flow from changes in belief, they foster changes in belief.[8] Of course, forcing a group of teachers to team together doesn't make them good or willing collaborators, but the teachers will never grasp what teaming can offer or learn how to collaborate if they don't try. Experimenting with a new behavior is often a prerequisite for new learning. Pressure thus helps to promote commitment, spurring the process by which we finally accept loss and reformulate our patterns of meaning.

There is no denying that pressure can cause casualties. The more intense and widespread the loss caused by an innovation, the less likely it is that every staff member will choose to embrace it or be able to achieve it. Some may prefer to leave; others may have to be let go. In virtually every other field but education employers see these consequences as inevitable. Corporations pursuing improved performance routinely take a "restructuring charge" to cover the cost of staff they've fired. Only in schools and religious institutions do we expect to accomplish major innovation without pain and turnover. Savvy school leaders, though not typically as hard-boiled as their corporate peers, nonetheless accept the necessity for this kind of triage. They anticipate that change will generate turnover. They know that turnover, especially when it is involuntary, sends shock waves through a faculty and, depending on the school and the context, through the larger school community, so they don't usually go out of their way to provoke it, but they don't avoid it when the need arises.

Support: Continuity, Contact, Time

Applying pressure, disconfirming people's views and beliefs about their performance, raising guilt and anxiety—these are necessary, especially at the outset of an innovation, but almost never sufficient. In my experience, disconfirmation and an intellectual agenda for change have never, by themselves, been enough to motivate participation. And if one only threatens people, they resist in all sorts of ways, overt and covert, conscious and unconscious. Disconfirmation can engender much fear and loathing—so much that people often dismiss the information, which lets them repress any anxiety or guilt. This is why, in many schools and organizations, disconfirming data about performance exist for a long time but are denied or devalued. To nourish innovation, pressure must be accompanied by support.

Support can be defined as anything that makes it easier to try the new. It can range from encouragement to training to financial incentives. It fosters what Schein calls psychological safety. It reduces the anxiety of change, the fear of trying something new. It begins by confirming for staff that the leader is committed not just to the change but to them. Thus, the early confrontation about the need for change must avoid humiliation, *ad hominem* attacks, blanket condemnations, and demands that people admit they were wrong. Change agents must demonstrate their caring and support, their commitment to work with staff to take the difficult steps in new learning. They must reaffirm connection and help make the change meaningful to people by finding the familiar in the new and strength amidst weakness. They must expect the grief and tolerate the mourning.

Most innovations can only flourish if staff adopt them actively, becoming vigorous, engaged participants. Hence, leaders must help those who are to implement change move from loss to commitment, from a letting go of the old to a true embrace of the new. Years ago I wrote that this principle, though especially vital, had for far too long been overlooked in school reform. Today it is, if anything, even more neglected. But for a long time now, the most promising school improvement proposals have called for fundamental changes in the ways teachers conceptualize teaching and learning, curriculum and assessment. These changes require active commitment and participation, not passive tolerance or partial engagement.

Fortunately, even though the obstacles to change are formidable, there are tendencies within the individual that support adaptation. Paradoxically, they emerge from pattern seeking and resistance. Although change usually causes loss, from such loss comes not only grief and despair but innovation.

Indeed, grief and despair are often sources of innovation. The strength of our tendency to seek patterns, the tenacity with which we cling to purposes and relationships, leads us at first to resist change, often fiercely, but also inclines us, ultimately, to accept it. We eventually come to accept the loss not merely as an event that has happened but as part of an expectable series of events.[9] Given the chance to revise and broaden the framework in which we understand things, our need to preserve continuity moves us to incorporate a change into our patterns of meaning and to adapt to it. Coping thus requires working out new meanings, making enough sense of the loss we have suffered so that we can come to accept new functions and assume new roles. This is a kind of grief work. The conditions that are required for adaptation are those necessary in resolving grief.

These begin with reaffirming continuity. Change agents tend to conceive of their improvements as substitutions—replacing something old, worse, and illogical with something new, better, and logical. But people cannot resolve their grief simply by substitution; they must work their way through it. They must learn to reformulate the purposes and attachments that are threatened by change.[10] This process is complex, both cognitively and emotionally. It needs continuity. People must be helped to link the new with the old, to see the future not as disconnected from the past but as related to it. Ideally, they need to see the future as fulfilling traditional values in new ways. This search involves a period—often lengthy—of distress and ambivalence as people try to grasp the full extent of what is being lost and modify their patterns of meaning to incorporate the new. This search cannot be hurried and each person must do it for himself. Efforts to jump-start change, to preempt opposition or conflict by thorough planning and rational explanation alone, are likely to be futile. For it is only through reworking again (and, often, again and again) our experience of loss and the necessity to adapt that we come to accept change and commit ourselves to something new.

To bear loss and invest in new ways of behaving, to move from bereavement toward commitment, to abandon old competencies and try new ones, people need help to graft new perceptions and priorities onto the roots of older ones. They almost always need a person, a leader, to embody the change and create the bridge between the old and the new, to help them relinquish what they hold dear so that they can move on. This can never be forced. It is best accomplished when the leader's vision overtly emphasizes continuity, making change more familiar by linking the future to the past and emphasizing existing strengths.

When leaders can explain change in clear, focussed terms and connect innovation to longstanding values that matter to constituents, reaffirming wherever possible the school's traditional principles and qualities, they help staff link the new with the old and bear the uncertainties and losses of change. Keith Shahan, reflecting on an exceptional career leading public and independent schools, sees this transitional help as defining leadership more generally. "Good leaders," he says, "develop a narrative for the organization, so that people understand where they have been, where they are, what they need to do to get where they need to go. Linking the values of an organization to the narrative and communicating it well is a pretty good job description for a leader."[11]

People's progress from loss to commitment benefits enormously from personal contact with the leader. Those who are being asked to implement change respond better when they have regular attention from, and access to, those who are responsible for it. This contact serves two key functions: the obvious one is to help in the learning of new skills and the troubleshooting of problems. The less obvious but equally important aspect is to assuage the very personal losses innovation provokes. Not least among these is the severing of personal attachments as people leave and relationships are altered, which in itself is a source of bereavement. A key way that teachers' needs for continuity can be sustained is by regular contact with a sympathetic principal who will acknowledge the distress they are experiencing even as she reconfirms the promise of change and reinforces the necessity and potential of the new skills required. Personal contact that is oriented toward both task performance *and* emotional adjustment greatly facilitates the adoption of innovation.

Even when support and contact are plentiful, grief is often slow to yield. Respecting people's need to process loss and fashion their own meanings out of change means allowing them sufficient time. Change is so highly personal that all who will be affected by it must have the chance to work it through, try it on, see how it fits, and discover what they can gain from it as well as what it will cost them.[12] This takes time. When we seek genuine commitment and changes in belief, the person doing the changing is in control of the transformation, not the architect of the change. Teachers must be permitted time to complain, to wish things were different, to long for the old days, to worry that they won't be able to manage the new approaches, and so on. This opportunity can't last forever, but if it is denied altogether, resistance simply goes underground and undermines the necessary change. The leader can't wait indefinitely, but she often has to wait longer than she imagined.

The Artful Balance

Unfortunately, neither continuity, nor personal contact, nor time for grief come naturally to many change agents. This was true even during the heyday of the school reform movements of the 1980s and 1990s, which were much more humane than the narrow, test-driven approaches favored today. Innovators tend to concentrate on the potential benefits of their recommendations and to overlook the effort and pain of adapting. They can easily assume a very moralistic tone: change is Right, the status quo is Wrong. Too often they don't acknowledge the loss provoked by innovation or attend to the grief of those it affects. They tend to be impatient to get on with progress and to see implementation as a matter of persuasion and power: one should explain the rational necessity for the change and then use appropriate combinations of carrot and stick to maneuver or, if necessary, compel compliance. But to rely on these alone is to overestimate the influence of the leader and underestimate the realities of adaptation.

It is also a self-defeating hubris. After all, reformers who press staff to innovate have already assimilated the reform and made sense of it for themselves. In Marris's terms, they have already worked out a reformulation of purposes and practices that makes sense to them, one that may have taken them a long time—and that, as they were working it out, may have caused them real distress. Denying others the opportunity to make a similar journey, criticizing them for not responding to explanations about change, dismissing their resistance or hesitation as ignorance or prejudice, expresses arrogance and contempt for the meaning of other people's lives.[13] This contempt, which denies people respect and the time to move through loss toward commitment, does little but intensify opposition and impede implementation.

The wisest change leaders don't make this mistake. Nor, as noted, do they simply await an intellectual immaculate conception that delivers spontaneous commitment. They convey two essential messages. The first is, "This is very serious, the risks of inaction are very real, and we must change." The second is, "I value you as people and I will help you get where we need to go." They thus straddle the fault line between pressure and support, change and continuity, confirming their commitment to the people who must accomplish the change even as they express their commitment to the change itself and urge them to act. No wonder Schein calls unfreezing "one of the most complex and artful of human endeavors."[14] Because we too often equate power with coercion, we fail to see that power need not be malignant but rather a means to fulfill a larger vision that takes into account the needs of most, if not all. Viewed in this way, it is quite compatible with support. In fact, the two are complementary, as Michael Fullan has noted: "Pressure without support leads to resistance and alienation; support without pressure leads to drift or waste of resources."[15] Successful innovation combines the right amount of both. Together, they respect the human need to find meaning in change and encourage the human capacity to adapt.

Chapter Four

The Fourth Secret

Bite Off What You Can Chew

Effective executives concentrate on the few major areas where
superior performance will produce outstanding results.

—Peter Drucker[1]

T O TRAVEL WIDELY IN GOOD SCHOOLS IS TO MEET MANY
talented, dedicated leaders who are in over their heads.
In terms not of their skills but of their goals. They are adept
at running their institutions but swamped by their commitments. They've embraced complex changes and lofty challenges that are far beyond their schools' reach. Overreaching,
however, is not just a trait of these leaders, it is de rigeur in
American education. Since at least the early 1980s it has been
one of the defining characteristics of school improvement in
the United States. The academic outcomes expected of schools
and the nonacademic responsibilities assigned to them have
mushroomed beyond anything anyone could have imagined

thirty years ago. This reach for greater height, depth, and breadth has become a source of purpose and pride for teachers and administrators committed not just to better instruction but to a vision of schooling as the institution that will fulfill the best of America's capacities and commitments. And it has become a heavy burden.

The remarkable range of reform movements and restructuring initiatives, together with other innovative efforts that accompanied them, led to powerful transformations in some schools and to broad, though not necessarily deep, shifts in the practices of a great many others. But they also multiplied the quantity and complexity of educators' work. And then came the current federally mandated testing mania, which has imposed requirements that undermine—indeed contradict— many of the very changes schools had been trying to implement. Meanwhile, a sharp decline in the developmental functioning of the family and other social institutions has caused a notable deterioration in students' readiness to be learners and parents' readiness to be good partners with the school. Delivering on all the goals and responsibilities has proved to be more than difficult. In schools of all kinds it has become a source of growing frustration and declining morale, posing a real challenge to leaders.

The savviest leaders I've met are committed to innovation and improvement, but in a no-nonsense, practical way. They know that the conventional wisdom in the field vastly exaggerates the potential (and hence the apparent failure) of schools to shape the lives of children. They work hard in the service of their goals but they know that there is a large—and widening—gap between ideals and needs on the one hand, and realities and resources on the other. And so they don't just work hard, they think hard—about how much and how fast, about what they and their schools can truly achieve, given the students and families they serve and the resources they command. The answers are sobering; they don't inspire easy optimism. But they don't engender apathy or hopelessness, either. They stimulate savvy leaders to focus their efforts and maximize their leverage.

School Is a Weak Treatment

Virtually all of the major reform movements of the past thirty years have emphasized twin commitments to excellence and equity. They have differed sharply about how they define these goals and the means for achieving them, but all have asserted in one way or another that transforming educational performance depends on setting and achieving high standards for all students. "High expectations" and "all children can learn" have become ubiquitous in school mission and vision statements, along with vows to develop in students leadership, character, a lifelong love of learning, technological literacy, and global awareness, as well as to celebrate diversity, and to close the achievement gap between the performance of African-American and Hispanic students and their white and Asian-American peers.

Academically, these commitments have meant, among other things, new approaches to curriculum and instruction, new applications of research into learning styles, new emphases on interdisciplinary work and on the school as a professional learning community, and new ways to integrate technology into instruction. They have also led to the proliferation of programs to improve students' communication and leadership skills, strengthen their character development, and prevent a wide range of social, medical, and psychological ills, including drug and alcohol abuse, eating disorders, stress, suicide, pregnancy, AIDS, bullying, racism, and sexism.

The consequences of all this have been, to put it mildly, challenging. They have left schools with a vastly overloaded improvement agenda, engaged in what I have long thought of as "simultaneous multiple improvement": a series of concurrent new initiatives, each competing for scarce dollars and time and for teachers' allegiance. Advancing on many fronts at once became a source of pride for many leaders, proof of being on the cutting edge(s). But we have now reached the point where the academic content that schools must cover between kindergarten and graduation is roughly twice what it was in the early 1960s. More and more topics must be taught sooner and faster. But sooner and faster are not enough; we also want higher and deeper. We want teachers to inculcate higher-order thinking skills and in-depth understandings of essential concepts, beginning at ever earlier ages. And we want broader. We want all this achieved with virtually all students, including the disadvantaged and the disabled. Together, all this makes a commitment that is truly noble. And hopelessly unrealistic. It ignores the most fundamental fact of educational life: *on the day seniors graduate from high school they have spent, on average, less than ten percent of their lives—and none of their formative first years—in school.*

People often react with disbelief to this statistic, but on their eighteenth birthday students have been alive for nearly 157,800 hours and have spent fewer than 13,000 (eight percent) of these in school. The maximum proportion imaginable would be about eighteen percent, which could theoretically be reached by highly engaged pupils if we were to credit them with perfect attendance from kindergarten on; count all their school-related activity (5,000 to 6,000 hours of homework, sports, extracurriculars, and so on); and exclude from our calculation the time they spend sleeping (roughly 53,000 hours). Schools, in short, must achieve everything they are to accomplish in a narrow slice of students' experience.

The underlying rationale for most of the change pressed upon schools discounts this ten-percent reality. In addition to emphasizing excellence and equity, the major school restructuring movements and initiatives of the past three decades have shared the assumption that schooling is a powerfully determinative influence on most children and that transforming schools will thus transform the lives and futures of students. This view has certainly been visible in the major federal initiatives: the now infamous 1983 report, *A Nation at Risk*, that wrongly predicted imminent economic decline in America because of so-called "a rising tide of mediocrity" in our schools; Goals 2000, under President George H. W. Bush, which proclaimed that within eleven years, U.S. students would, among other things, lead the world in math and science; and No Child Left Behind (NCLB), under President George W. Bush, with its even more wildly unrealistic goal (all students will be "proficient" by 2014).

More broadly, most school critics and reformers of the past several decades have reduced "education" to "schooling." This is a serious error. What children learn in school is but a part of their total education. And even when we focus just on school and academics, whether children learn does not, as the psychologist Mihaly Csikszentmihalyi points out, "depend primarily on what happens in school, but on the experiences, habits, values, and ideas they acquire from the environment in which they live."[2] School is a part of that environment, but by no means the most significant. Indeed, viewed in the context of a student's whole growing up, schooling is, *by itself*, a "weak treatment," in James Gallagher's phrase. Gallagher argues that school is responsible, on average, for, at best, twenty-five percent of a student's total outcome.[3] This strikes me as a generous estimate, one that is nearly three times the actual time spent in school for most students, but let us accept it. It is not an insignificant number, but it leaves school still far from being profoundly determinative. For my part, I have no doubt that schooling has a real impact on many students and is life-changing for others, even life-saving for some. But in the lives and learning of most children, schooling is an important but minority influence.

School's narrow time window alone would make a sharp rise in performance expectations across a broad range of academic and nonacademic domains a difficult challenge. Unfortunately, this rise has been accompanied by a sharp drop in student readiness. It's not just the quantity of students' non-school time that looms so large, but its quality. What happens in the rest of their lives is increasingly undermining the habits, norms, and values that nurture academic achievement and community. Schools have always depended upon parents and other societal inputs to produce and sustain school readiness in children. (Remember Goals 2000's first commitment, that all children in America would start school ready to learn? Consider how achievement would improve if this condition alone were met—and how helpless schools are to guarantee it.) More and more, a school that takes seriously what we once considered basic American values—be honest, work hard, delay gratification, practice the Golden Rule, and so on—is on its own, a countercultural institution. Models of those values seem ever harder to find among politicians, businesspeople, athletes, and even, unfortunately, the clergy.

The chief challenge for schools, however, begins at home. Contrary to what many critics of American education claim, we don't have a crisis in schooling, we have something much worse: a crisis in childrearing. What have deteriorated most over thirty years are not the skills of our teachers but the lives of our students. The supports vital to good development (hence to schooling) are in free fall. The symptoms of the crisis—a continuing decline in the academic achievement, work ethic, and civility of many of our youth—appear vividly at school, but they begin well before it and extend well beyond it. Schools, even those that serve their students poorly, are much more its victims than its perpetrators.

In 1992, in *America's Smallest School: The Family*, Paul Barton and Richard Coley forecast the failure of Goals 2000 if it ignored the obvious: that the family is the cradle of learning, the essential socializing institution. It was already clear, they pointed out, that student achievement improves when there are two parents in the home; when children are well cared for and feel secure; when the family environment is intellectually stimulating; when parents encourage self-regulation and perseverance; when they limit TV, monitor homework, and ensure regular school attendance.[4] All of these are vital to producing and sustaining a school-ready, motivated student. And the evidence was already strong that in most of these areas the family was failing.

Today, the evidence is ubiquitous, and not just in our worst schools. Across the country, in communities of all kinds, more and more children arrive at school less ready to learn. Not less intelligent, less ready to be students; that is, less able to form a line, listen to others, share materials, persevere at tasks; more likely to see adult expectations as negotiable; more focussed on immediate gratification; less considerate of others. The fundamentals that make it possible for schools and teachers to influence children—attendance, attention, cooperation, courtesy, industry, responsibility—are all in broad decline. Meanwhile, their parents assert less authority over them and are themselves less respectful of the school's authority and more likely to challenge its decisions, to expect the school to make exceptions to its policies. Increasingly, they want the school to prepare the path for the child instead of the child for the path. These trends, which occur among families from all socioeconomic levels, pose a powerful obstacle to any school seeking to accelerate student performance. They make it ever harder to improve outcomes, even when schools do raise their standards and upgrade instruction. At the ordinary, every-day end of today's spectrum, students are more difficult to reach and teach, their concentration and perseverance more fragile, their language and behavior more challenging. At the catastrophic end lie the massacres at Columbine and other schools. Children are being left behind everywhere in all sorts of ways that schools can do little about.

Savvy school leaders are practical. They know that no matter what they might wish or legislators might mandate, their schools cannot hope to accomplish the bloated agenda thrust upon them. They want their schools to be the absolute best they realistically can. These leaders know this means choosing and concentrating. They don't try to fulfill everyone else's agenda. They aren't inflexible and they make compromises where they must, but they are clear and focussed.

Clarity

Studies of high-performing systems show that their leaders provide direction that is clear, strong, and unambivalent—not dictatorial, but definite—that although leadership styles may vary among such organizations, within each it tends to be remarkably consistent.[5] This clarity brings many advantages. The first is to foster trust, the sine qua non of leadership. When leaders are consistent, straightforward, and firm, staff find them reliable and predictable. They know what is expected and what to expect; they know how people are to behave and how performance is to be measured. High levels of trust raise confidence and competence and make the workplace more compatible, which in turn makes people more likely to cooperate and better able to tolerate stress.

Clarity also fosters commitment and garners attention. Goals cannot be shared unless they are understood—none of us can invest in a vision we don't grasp—and a consistent, lucid formulation of goals and their rationale over time creates clarity throughout an organization about broad purposes and immediate objectives.[6] As I suggested in Chapter Three, when faced with change, people need to know *why, what,* and *how*: why they must change, to what, and how this will be accomplished. They need to grasp for themselves the necessity of changing, or at least grasp their leaders' perception of the necessity. The leader must make the case for change, clarifying "where we are and why we can't stay here." This requires a clear, candid, forceful diagnosis of the issues the school is encountering—changes in the environment, problems in performance—and of the risks of inaction. From this emerges a course for change, a vision of "what we need to become."[7]

A predisposition toward clarity reflects an approach to leadership that is primarily directive, rather than an emphasis on situational flexibility or bottom-up democracy. It does not discourage staff engagement and participation, but it assumes that the leader's vision is "the magnetic north that sets the compass course,"[8] that the leader must be at the forefront of framing the change and making it comprehensible. This kind of presence by a leader provides a basic confidence for staff and helps to concentrate their effort and attention. These are essential in any organization, but especially schools because the goals of improvement initiatives are often broad, diffuse, and multifaceted (hence hard to understand) and because reformers often disagree so much about the remedies. The ultimate goal of clarity is a shared community-wide consensus about values and goals, but this is truly an ultimate goal, not a beginning condition. The impetus for the goal almost always begins from the top, or very near it; rarely does it well up from below.

Before continuing, I must emphasize two things that clarity does *not* mean: rigidity and abrasiveness. Savvy leaders may be persistent, but they are not blind. They will modify an approach or a timetable—even a goal—if significant external events or institutional realities (such as major budget cuts) make the pursuit of a priority impossible. But they don't do this lightly or merely to avoid discomfort (letting a teacher evade an important requirement just to reduce friction). Nor does being clear and specific entail rudeness, harshness, condescension, or taking away teachers' discretion. Good leaders aren't arbitrary; they don't insist on their way peremptorily. If necessary, they do insist, but they begin by asking and listening and explaining. And they work hard to keep discussions and decisions focussed on issues—curriculum, say, or student outcomes—rather than personalities.

Focus

Clarity's corollary is focus. One might theoretically be clear about a long roster of goals, but the longer the roster the harder it is to understand, let alone fulfill. The most effective leaders follow Peter Drucker's famous advice, cited at the start of this chapter, to concentrate their efforts on a few key targets—advice that has found consistent confirmation for more than thirty years: leaders of successful organizations target their energies, centering their time and effort on a short list of key issues, even if this means ignoring others. They are focussed on their goals and, by actively communicating their judgments about what is important, bring focus to staff behavior. Even in organizations that are not pursuing major new innovations, there are always many issues that need to be solved, many projects competing for attention. Successful leaders, as Peter Vaill notes, "know what few things are important, and in their statements and actions they make these priorities known."[9] I have always seen this a little differently: these leaders *decide* what few things are important. What's important is not necessarily innate or inevitable, written in the stars and discernible only to a leader with special insight. What's important is chosen by a leader and then pursued with a vigor and skill that brings success and makes its importance ultimately seem inevitable. Thus, the new head of an independent secondary school, though dismayed to find a range of serious shortcomings, was clear about where the school would concentrate first:

> There was so much more to do here than I was told when I applied for this job. Athletics were weaker—most of our teams were perennial losers, which damaged student morale; curriculum was more disjointed—teachers taught whatever they wanted without any attention to the larger scope and sequence of a student's experience; environmental sensitivity was abysmal—we didn't recycle anything; and diversity was an empty shell—we did little to recruit, support, and retain faculty and students of color. I told folks we were going to tackle all of these, but diversity was first on my list. Of all the shortcomings I found, it was the most glaring. I devoted my first in-service day to reviewing our existing diversity efforts and exploring areas for improvement. We began to make plans and identify areas where we needed to make changes.

This head's first year wasn't only about diversity. She began to talk with department chairs about a full-blown curriculum review, she charged a team to begin planning ways the school could start going green, and she hired a new athletic director and asked him to start an assessment of their whole athletic and physical education program. But these projects would all develop and emerge over the following several years. "Diversity," she says, "was front and center until we got it much more deeply ingrained into the way we live and work at this school."

A leader who focusses in this way acknowledges that there are more issues than the school can tackle, more worthy initiatives than it can undertake at one time, and that the school must therefore decide the relative importance of each. Because few people can accomplish multiple complex changes at once, choosing where to concentrate is crucial—especially in schools, which are the object of so many different improvement efforts. Even if the agenda for change results from a truly democratic, collaborative planning process, someone will need to serve as its overseer and navigator. Someone will need to monitor progress and guide course corrections. That someone is the leader. If superintendents are not definite about which program or which constituency has top priority, principals' daily decisions in their schools will not show a consistent direction. Similarly, if principals are not definite, teachers' daily decisions in their classrooms will also fail to show a consistent direction.

What does focus mean in practice? *One major change at a time per person and per work group.* As sensible and straightforward as this maxim seems, I've encountered few schools anywhere that respect it. Yet one at a time is the rule of thumb in corporate settings: an innovation with six major components typically has six separate teams; each particular work group concentrates on only one. This does not mean innovation must be narrow. Far from it. The reform may be wide ranging and multifaceted. But the more complex the project, the clearer and more compatible its priorities must be; the more its elements must fit coherently under one conceptual roof and make combined sense to those who implement it. If it has multiple dimensions, individuals must not be expected to master all of these at once. The more a project aims at deep, thorough, cultural change, the fewer companions or competitors it must have.

When I recommend focus to educators, most agree readily—they know the futility of the bloated improvement agenda better than anyone—but cannot imagine how they might even begin to press seriously for it. Teacher audiences ask, "Do you recommend this to administrators?" Administrative audiences ask, "Do you recommend this to school boards and state officials?" Lately, they've all been asking, "Do you recommend this to the NCLB people in Washington?" Given the forces arrayed against focus—the legislative and regulatory mandates, the diverse reform con- stituencies and special interest groups—their doubt is under- standable. Innovation triage is hard. There are, however, at least three practical ways school leaders can push for focus.

The first is to advocate strongly and proactively with the relevant constituencies *for* purposes one values rather than *against* those one doesn't. Savvy leaders tend to control the terms of debate by asserting their key themes over and over. Being so positively focussed on their goals, they emphasize not just the external rationale of the effort but its intrinsic rewards—how exciting, how promising, even how enjoyable it is. This creates interest and invites participation.[10] In the same way, they enact the principle that an organization's mis- sion and strategy begin with its strengths, not its deficits or the apparent wishes of its "market." To solve most problems, a school needs to draw on its talents and in many cases will achieve greater success sooner by actively seeking to maximize what it does well. (More on this in Chapter Six.)

The second is that savvy leaders ask not just, "What do we need to start doing?" but also, "What can we stop doing?" An elementary principal in one of the nation's premier school dis- tricts once told me that their district's motto should be, *You name it, we start it.* "We've never finished anything," he said. "We just keep creating new ideas and programs." He had no interest in pursuing—or pretending to pursue—initiatives that had run out of steam or would siphon energy from his key pri- orities. When pressured from above into simultaneous multiple improvement, a good principal or division head will confront—civilly, gently, even—the lack of focus. Thus, when faced with a demand to do something new, one asks, "And what shall we stop doing?" When the answer is, "Nothing. We want you to add this to the list," one asks, "How did you think we might do that?" When the answer is, "I know you'll be creative," one replies, "Actually, I think that will interfere with our ability to fulfill our existing commitments. Where should we concentrate?" When this fails to produce a change of heart and the new demand is imposed, one does one's best. Then, at year's end, when the criticism is, "You didn't accomplish the new priority," one doesn't apologize, one agrees: "Yes, that's right. As I feared, our agenda is too full. I think we need to target our top priority and really go after it."

If there is little hope of paring down the agenda, a remaining option is to stretch out timelines of individual items, especially for recurrent improvement projects, such as curriculum upgrades. These can be shifted from an annual cycle to a two-year cycle (planning new math units one year and taking the second to debug and modify these, then moving on to review science or social studies and giving that effort two years, and so on). In my experience, most school improvement projects would benefit from having their time lines extended. Indeed, I'm always surprised when I encounter a school that has allocated sufficient time for the implementation of a major innovation.

A Little Too Much May Be Just Enough

Biting off just what you can chew may seem too cautious. Many writers on organizational innovation and proponents of school reform believe change agents should overreach.

They argue that change agents often have a brief window in which to accomplish their agenda and that especially when the institution is entrenched in its outlook and practices, seeking incremental improvements will take forever. They acknowledge that leaders who pursue a full-bore approach to change often fail to achieve their full agenda. But, they claim, these leaders achieve more than they otherwise would. Even if they don't last long they change the school's essential dynamic and force it to come to grips with new realities. Plus, the effort seems more noble and inspiring. "A man's reach must exceed his grasp," in Robert Browning's famous phrase, "or what's a heaven for?"

I am glad to yield—slightly—on this point. I do not want to recommend excessive caution—indeed, the next chapter urges boldness—but I have never seen a school successfully implement multiple major innovations. I have seen leaders who took such an approach inspire much fear and loathing and I've seen many of them be fired and most of the rest give up in dismay. The savviest school leaders know that the longer the roster of goals and the more ambitious the individual targets, the less likely any will be achieved. They realize that they can't succeed if they push themselves and their teachers to accomplish the impossible; everyone burns out. But they also know that they can't succeed if they simply accept the status quo as unchangeable; everyone gives up. The art is to combine reach and realism. We will explore this concept further in Chapter Seven. Here we can note that savvy leaders don't abandon their commitments but that they also don't ignore psychological and organizational realities. They are committed to high standards, for example, but not in the standard ways—not in the simplistic, absolutist fashion that has become the norm. They know that historically schools have always reflected society more than they have shaped it and this will continue to be the case—the ten-percent window alone virtually guarantees this. Defining their own high standards, they keep reminding their teachers of both the challenge and the opportunity in working with today's students. They expect progress to be incremental and they don't ignore small gains against long odds. They set an example of perseverance, but not of perfectionism. And, as we will see in Chapter Six, they do for teachers what the best teachers do for students: they make it safe to try; they honor effort; and they celebrate meaningful growth, small and large, whenever it occurs.

Chapter Five

The Fifth Secret

Be Your Best, Bold Self

[P]eople would much rather follow individuals they can count on, even when they disagree with their viewpoint, than people they agree with but who shift their position frequently.

—Warren Bennis[1]

ABOUT NOW, MANY READERS MAY BE THINKING, "ALL WELL and good, all these recommendations in preceding chapters to be assertive, choose, clarify, focus, and so on, but how would I actually get away with any of this?" Indeed, the trends in educational policy and governance have been moving the other way, hemming leaders in rather than freeing them up, larding their responsibility while limiting their authority. So the answer to the question involves a sharp irony: as the pressures grow, so does the latitude to lead. Of course, no leaders anywhere are free to do just as they wish. All must learn to compromise, bend, soft-pedal—even, at times, backpedal. This has always been true in schools, especially public schools. It is even more true now that so much of the nation's educational agenda is dictated by law and regulation and that an ethos of participation—teacher and parent empowerment, shared decision making, servant leadership— has become so widespread in the writing and thinking about school reform and improvement.

But few leaders are ultimately rewarded for abandoning their commitments, which only dismays their supporters and emboldens their opponents, or for scurrying to be all things to all constituencies, which only makes them harder to understand and follow. And the liberating truth, which savvy leaders illustrate, is that most school leaders have more freedom and leeway than they use. In part this is because the very conditions that are making school leadership so arduous are driving people out of the field, thus increasing the leverage of those who remain. School leadership has become, at this writing, a seller's market. But it is also because asserting strength builds strength. As I noted in Chapter Two, people everywhere—all of us—long to be well led. Not bossed, led. As we have just seen, leaders with the courage of their convictions and the capacity to make meaning invite and inspire followers. But they don't do so through the conventional paths that have come to stand for good leadership. They do it by clarifying their commitments and maximizing their strengths, by being the best of who they are.

Pleasing and Power

As Chapter One suggested, leadership is too often seen as requiring maximal flexibility, an approach that too often leaves leaders running from pillar to post trying to be all things to all people. In education this tendency is especially wide-spread. Its roots certainly lie in the advice leaders are given in books they read and workshops they attend, but that advice has a special resonance for educators because of their very makeup: most are born pleasers. As a group, they tend to be highly conflict avoidant. They generally like people and want to be liked. As Chapter Three noted, they are, after all, people who thrive in—and in many ways prefer—the company of children and adolescents and who try to look for the best in them. They wish to help, nurture, foster, inspire, and encourage. And they have a real gift for guilt. They suffer from a condition I think of as "closet omnipotence," the belief that they should be all things to all people and should displease no one. The mere hint that they have failed to meet a student's need or caused someone distress is likely to make them feel anxious and guilty. This stimulates high levels of dedication, but can leave them feeling chronically inadequate and lessen their appetite and ability to assert themselves with other adults.

Of course, teachers who become administrators develop an increased capacity to tolerate negativity and conflict because they inevitably have to make unpopular decisions and because they encounter the dilemmas reviewed in Chapter Two. Most have, for example, not renewed a low-performing teacher, sometimes in dramatic circumstances. But in my experience most dislike and delay doing so. They don't want to displease, cause pain, face a confrontation, or endure the anger of the "victim's" colleagues. Even with regard to less controversial matters, many are prone to sugarcoating or minimizing bad news. Underneath, their closet omnipotence and gift for guilt remain strong.

This tendency is so entrenched that it keeps many from advocating for themselves and acting on opportunities to increase their leverage. I have been struck, for example, by the number of principals who have been unwilling to exploit the seller's market. In the past few years I've listened to dozens of principals complain bitterly about being micromanaged by the school board, unfairly criticized by parents, or unsupported by the superintendent. And I've listened, too, to a litany of reasons why they felt they couldn't or shouldn't voice these concerns. On a number of these occasions I've known of a principalship opening in a neighboring community (no need to sell the house and move) and have asked whether they've considered applying. The response has almost always been no. "I couldn't do that," they say, or "I love my school," or "I've hired most of this faculty," or "They'd never forgive me." Almost none were even willing to explore the possibility of changing, or to tell their superintendent that they were considering exploring openings elsewhere.

I wasn't suggesting that they should move, nor am I recommending here that principals should change schools more often. My point is that principals and school heads (and, for that matter, superintendents) have increased power to *lead*—power that they are too often reluctant to use. Increasingly, the school needs the leader more than the leader needs the school. Until running a school once again becomes a manageable job with reasonable expectations—a distant prospect indeed—the blunt reality for those willing to serve is this: *if you can stand the abuse, you're guaranteed lifetime employment.* Some school or district somewhere will need you.

From this blunt reality flows an equally straightforward implication: *use your leverage*, or, as I often think of it, *do what you want and let 'em come get you.* By this I don't mean be selfish, capricious, or high-handed, I mean do what matters most to you, pursue your priorities, be true to your commitments. Invite, encourage, urge, and ultimately insist that others follow. This is what savvy leaders do. They know that exceptional organizational performance requires assertive leadership, not pleasing everyone. Almost all the successful leaders I know are good at engaging and listening to their people, but they nurture and project their influence. They are not overweening but they are definitely not wallflowers. At an immediate, personal level, they assert themselves because they enjoy doing so. They couldn't attract followers if they didn't. In the same way that good teachers like to teach, good leaders like to lead—not to control people but to make things happen. Describing "the charge" he gets out of leading, a superintendent told me, "I complain about my burdens like everyone else, but I love solving problems, and I especially love being able to help other people solve problems."

This orientation is fortunate, because there is a whole range of essential functions—practical, political, managerial, ceremonial, strategic—that require a chief. Every school needs a "head," someone to focus it, tend it, represent it, and speak for it—someone to do for the school what a teacher does for a class. Just as a teacher sees the forest of the classroom, whereas students see the trees, so principals see the forest of the school, whereas teachers usually see the trees. The difference is not one of intelligence but of perspective and role. Someone has to embody the institution, set its course, monitor its progress, troubleshoot its problems, and manage its people. This is a leader's work. Most of us have at some time been part of an organization with weak or incompetent leadership that fails to fulfill these tasks and have seen how it drains energy, invites dysfunction, and inhibits performance. Without a sufficient level of savvy and integrity at the top, efforts to grow, to innovate, and to empower staff are largely irrelevant.

In my experience, the best school leaders are not interested in being influential to gratify their egos. They have strong convictions about how things ought to be in school, they concentrate tenaciously on a few key goals, they generally prefer directness and specificity in their dealings with constituents about these goals, and they exemplify their commitment in their behavior. This helps them solve one of the thorniest problems in leadership, the "vision thing," as George H. W. Bush called it. Savvy leaders avoid the bloated vision and mission rituals that predominate in schools and build instead a true, shared sense of purpose.

Purposing

The importance of purpose to organizational performance is as widely enshrined in education as in any sphere of American public life. Virtually every school in America has a mission statement. Many also have a vision statement, and a number have gone for the trifecta, adopting a set of core values as well. The three overlap: *mission* refers to an organization's reason for being; *vision* to its future direction; and *core values* to its underlying beliefs and guiding principles. Often, the three are accompanied by or folded into a strategic plan. Many public school districts and most independent schools engage in regular strategic planning, a process in which they revisit mission, vision, and values; assess strengths and weaknesses, opportunities and threats; and set priorities for future direction. All are part of what Peter Vaill calls *purposing*, which he defines as a "continuous stream" of leadership actions that fosters "clarity, consensus, and commitment regarding the organization's basic purposes."[2]

What matters most about any kind of purposing is not which commitments it proclaims but how much they matter, especially how much they matter to those who must implement them. The main function of purposing is to inspire people and to concentrate their efforts on the pursuit of a common agenda. But for all the effort schools expend on purposing, it's still unusual to find a school where all faculty members can even tell you what the mission or vision statement says. This despite the fact that a broad, participatory, grass roots process is supposed to produce a widespread "sense of ownership" in the outcome. In practice, involving all the stakeholders usually results in trying to accommodate all their views and thus leads to documents that, as I have suggested, are overlong and overpromise. Most are unprioritized wish lists full of lofty goals and qualities to which the school aspires (not strengths that truly define it). The lists, brimming with commitments to academic excellence for all students; to athletic excellence; to preparing students for a globalized world; to instilling a lifelong love of learning, a respect for human differences, and an appreciation of the arts; to teaching technological literacy, and so on, all ignore the limits imposed by the school's ten-percent slice of students' lives. The short form of most would be *heal the sick and raise the dead.*

Perhaps nowhere do purposing flaws arise more prominently than when a school or district undertakes strategic planning. The process is now ubiquitous, widely accepted as a hallmark of sound school governance. Periodically taking a fresh look at realities and challenges can certainly engage everyone's attention in a constructive way, helping to renew energy and commitment, as well as identifying specific help-ful action steps. And many board members and others who participate in the process often seem to enjoy it. But standard strategic planning is beset by serious built-in fallacies. As its most trenchant critic, Henry Mintzberg, has famously observed, the term itself is an oxymoron: planning is *analysis*, strategy is *synthesis*, and the former cannot produce the latter. Planning gets you a plan, not necessarily a strategy. It consists of studying problems and possibilities, choosing goals, breaking these into action steps, and spelling out the expected results of each step. Strategy, however, is "an integrated perspective of the enterprise, a not-too-precisely articulated vision of direction" that is compelling but not rigid, simple rather than detailed.[3]

This fundamental flaw is accompanied by others. Strategic planners typically assume that the world will remain static while the plan is created and then behave as anticipated during its lifespan, even though the world is changing so fast that the plan easily ends up out of date or irrelevant. They also typically assume that the keys to strategy lie in objective measures of hard data, and so ignore the "decidedly soft underbelly" of the organization, even when this underbelly is crucial to choosing the right organizational direction—as it most certainly is in a school, which is so dependent on human capital and relationships.[4] Moreover, the priorities most schools and districts end up adopting are, like the aspirational goals of their mission statements, highly predictable: faculty recruitment and retention; facilities; technology; diversity—and improved financial strength to support all this. And as planning has grown more popular, the plans have tended to increase in rigidity and size. I think of six recent plans from well-known independent schools. The shortest translates its goals and objectives into 40 action steps; the largest, into 207. What more fitting bookend for a heal-the-sick-and-raise-the-dead mission statement than a choke-a-horse strategic plan?

There are exceptions, of course. Not all plans suffer these flaws. And there are some situations in which a full, traditional planning process can still make good sense, such as when a new leader follows a long-serving predecessor, or when there has been significant turmoil in the school or a serious downturn in morale, enrollment, or finance. Some veteran independent school heads have grown adept at managing the planning process so that it emphasizes their priorities. But I know many who would agree with the head who once thought planning "the very essence of leadership," but to whom it now seems "a ritual with minimal relevance to how this school operates and the actual problems I have to solve."

Top-Down and Bottom-Up

Given all this, most savvy leaders I know reject the standard approaches to purposing. They endorse the ideal of participation and empowerment and planning, but not slavishly. They want to optimize collective involvement, but not at the expense of their core commitments. They expect to play a primary role in shaping their school's agenda and they see empowerment as a later outcome, not a starting condition, one that involves responsibility, not license. They seek an optimal, not a maximal, level of participation. They know that making change often requires, as we have seen, power and pressure, and that it needs a framework they must provide. They will not sacrifice substance for process. They do not abandon traditional authority; they use it judiciously, building involvement as they can in a variety of informal as well as formal ways, inviting participation where it seems most relevant and practical, but asserting themselves as they must. They provide a binary leadership that is both top-down and bottom-up. In this way they avoid the pitfalls that can turn purposing and decision making into quagmires, they garner support, build coalitions, inspire commitment, and help school communities deepen the commitment on which improvement depends.

In this they resemble their corporate peers. In the business world, leaders typically adopt what Edgar Schein calls a "strong vision" approach. The chief executive spells out a definite picture of where the organization must go and how it must get there. He may then embark on a broad effort to communicate this vision to the workforce and may engage staff in open discussion about it. But he sets the course. Take-charge turnaround leaders and so-called "transformational" leaders almost always adopt such a stance. They stake out the goals and make the case, they inspire and encourage, they goad and insist. They also listen and, as appropriate, modify. And when all else fails, they fire and hire. In many ways, this approach is a natural fit for savvy leaders with clear priorities.

Of course in schools, particularly public schools, leaders are not as free as their corporate counterparts. They may have equally strong convictions, but they have weaker leverage. Nonetheless, almost all the celebrated school change agents I know or about whom I've read are essentially strong vision practitioners. They have definite, distinct priorities, they make the case for these forcefully and persuasively, and in so doing they enlist support. Even though they have much less formal power than their corporate peers, they find ways to move their schools, relying on passion, clarity, and courage.

It is not ideas by themselves that enlist participation and invigorate performance, it is leaders with ideas. It is the personal impact of a mission or vision or plan, not just its intellectual content, that moves people. As former IBM chairman Louis Gerstner told a reporter, people must "buy in with their hearts and their bellies, not just their minds."[5] Authentic leaders are passionate, which doesn't mean they are necessarily loud or charismatic, it means they are committed and they convey this commitment by what they do as well as by what they say. They don't hide their interests. They concentrate their time and energy on activities related to their priorities. I know principals who will skip districtwide administrative meetings if these conflict with in-school meetings that are central to their key goals. When challenged, they will agree candidly that they care about x more than y, not denigrating y, but confirming their commitment to x.

In this regard, I've always treasured an anecdote that I heard years ago about a principal so focussed on turning around a low-performing, impoverished urban elementary school that she rarely replied to the endless stream of paperwork sent out by the district's central office. She wanted to begin each week able to be present with and focussed on her teachers, students, and parents. So each Friday she put anything that had arrived that week from the central office in a bag, which she dated and threw in her closet (this was long before e-mail; everything came in hard copy). If the district never inquired about any of the items, she ignored them. If the district called to say it hadn't received some mandatory reply from her, she would ask, "When did you send that?" find the document, and respond. Keeping her closet full kept her time free for her priorities.

Every bit as important as passion is clarity, not just about goals but decision making. Chapters Three and Four have explored the importance of the leader's being clear about goals. It is equally important to be clear about how decisions are made. In a strong vision scenario, the leader not only makes the case but also plots the course and announces it. In a more collaborative model she engages the staff in plotting the course. This is where clarity about decision making is crucial. In a school, as in any organization, there are a range of decisions to be made each year. They fall along a continuum from more leader centered to more participatory. Some, like hiring, can be made, if a leader wishes, through a collective process; others, like firing, cannot. As Figure 5.1 illustrates, at one extreme the leader has full control, decides alone, and simply announces the decision. At the other, staff have wide latitude to decide things on their own; the leader's vote may not count more than anyone else's. In between are a range of options: the leader presents a tentative decision

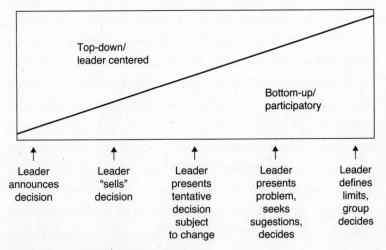

Figure 5.1. Decision-Making Continuum

Source: Adapted from Tannenbaum and Schmidt (1991).

subject to change based upon staff input, the leader offers a range of options and lets staff choose, and so on. The best leaders tend to be clear about where key decisions lie. It is a powerful source of their credibility.

Most of us hate to be told that a decision lies near the right (participatory) edge of the continuum, only to discover that it actually lies far to the left. Knowing how much weight our views will have makes a huge difference, even when we wish our views would weigh more heavily than the leader permits. The best leaders are adept at deciding who needs to be involved and when.[6] They are clear with staff about *who* is making *which* decisions and *how*. As a very successful independent school head told me years ago, "I want my teachers to know how their input will matter. I'm glad to involve them and to explain myself, but I don't get bogged down in process and when the decision is going to be mine I don't pretend otherwise. And they don't want me to." What she offers is not perfect parity, but genuine clarity. I've never met a faculty that didn't welcome this.

Reform-minded educators committed to participatory leadership often ask if I haven't encountered schools where decision making is largely conducted on the right side of the continuum, where much governance is broadly shared and where faculty are genuinely empowered. I have encountered such schools, but very, very few. And in every single one of these schools there has been a powerful principal, someone with passion and presence (that is, with conviction and confidence, not necessarily flamboyance), someone who seems competent enough to make *any* system of governance work. More often than not the principal has been a key architect of the participation-empowerment structure. Some of these principals are more charismatic than others, some hold more firmly to a "first among equals" status. But I have never known, and cannot imagine, a school in which participation and empowerment flourish over time without a strong leader.

What About Those Weaknesses?

In making the case for greater boldness I am not arguing that leaders are infallible and should do as they please. But as I noted in Chapter One, leaders of high-performing organizations know what they believe in and what they're good at, and they pursue the former through the latter. Are they aware of their weaknesses? Absolutely. Do they dwell on these? No. They know that any way of leading, like any way of being, has strengths and weaknesses, and that the two are almost always inseparable, reverse sides of a coin. A no-nonsense task master may be adept at crisis management but be too hard on people at other times. A calm consensus builder may promote rich collaboration but be too soft on holding people accountable. Successful leaders are prepared to live with the trade-offs. Ask a savvy corporate CEO to describe his leadership. Point out that he seems to do lots of x but very little y or z. He agrees. He doesn't get embarrassed. He doesn't wince and wonder where he can find a workshop on y and z. He says, "We're an x kind of place" or, "I'm good at x." Asked what he does about y and z, he says, "I hire it in others" or "I compensate when I need to."

This approach to leadership reflects a fundamental acceptance of the stability of personality and the limits on both personal change and on the leader's power. It acknowledges that interpersonal style is not something we can put on and take off, at least not in any consistent, authentic way. It also acknowledges that successful leadership depends on goodness of fit much more than changes in approach—a crucial point that contradicts much of the rosy writing on leadership. Every successful leader I've met was clear and focussed, but so were some who weren't successful. It's possible to be a good, savvy administrator in the wrong job at the wrong time. It's possible for external events—budgetary, political, cultural—to undermine one's efforts and initiatives, to dramatize one's weaknesses. Some leaders are ideally suited to conservative schools that want only slow, incremental improvement, and others to schools in need of thorough change. The essential question for the practitioner is, *Am I the kind of leader this school (or district) needs now?* not, *Can I become the kind of leader this school (or district) needs now?* To most savvy leaders this is simply a fact of life.

Approaching leadership this way does not deny the importance of learning and growth. On the contrary, it embodies a fundamental truth about both: it is always easier to build on a strength than to attack a weakness. I know a tiny handful of school heads, principals, and superintendents who have successfully made major adjustments in their approaches that helped them improve their capacities to lead their schools or districts. When any leader can manage this I'm delighted. But I know many, many more who have fruitlessly tried—sometimes over a period of years—to become something they're not, making themselves and their schools miserable. The savvy approach is to begin by extending existing competence. A simple way to start is to make a list of your strengths and a list of your weaknesses and ask several colleagues you trust to assess and edit both. Your weaknesses will probably be the flip side of your strengths. Post the strengths list where you'll see it regularly and now and then, when it catches your eye, ask yourself, How might I do a little more of one of those?

To repeat, it is important to be aware of your weaknesses, and there is nothing wrong with addressing them, provided this is not the chief way you try to improve. To do so is to succumb to a futile perfectionism that has dogged school leadership for far too long and is ultimately self-defeating.

Although it is true that leaders who maximize their strengths don't always succeed, that they occasionally find themselves bad fits for their current positions and need to find others, they greatly improve their odds of succeeding. The current harsh climate of school life makes the need for assertive, engaging leadership greater than ever. Those who can be their best, bold selves are uniquely ready to answer this need in a way that inspires confidence, builds common ground, confirms the meaningfulness of the work, and gives schools a fighting chance to master the challenges they face.

Chapter Six

The Sixth Secret

Nourish to Flourish

Leaders get the best from others not by building fires under people but by building the fire within them.

—James Kouzes and Barry Z. Posner[1]

I MAGINE A SCHOOL COMMITTED TO DISCOURAGING LEARNING and growth. Let's call it Perverse Academy (PA). What is the simplest, most effective way for PA to pursue its goal? By accentuating the negative and ignoring the positive. Its teachers would begin the school year by taking a detailed inventory of their students' weaknesses and would then hammer the students about these for the next ten months, organizing the entire curriculum around the students' shortcomings and dwelling on these daily. And during this time they would withhold not only praise for progress but also any acknowledgment for trying. The tagline on the school's Web site would be something like, "The PA Way: Dramatizing flaws, disregarding effort, discounting strengths."

Absurd? Of course. Out of the question? Only for students. Not for faculty. In the vast majority of schools I've visited, something not too unlike the PA Way is the norm for adults. Educators in most good schools observe a broad double standard, lavishing recognition and encouragement on students, while starving themselves of these essential nutrients. They help students not just to correct their weaknesses but to build on their strengths. For themselves, however, they focus firmly on their shortcomings.

Before we go any further, a quick definition: by "recognition" I mean "praise" and "validation." Recognition obviously includes the celebrating of accomplishment. But it also includes the honoring of effort. And it begins—and often ends—with the acknowledging of basic truths about a person's or an organization's situation, especially when these truths thwart effort and weaken outcomes. Above all, it confirms for people the value of their work and thus makes that work more meaningful and rewarding to them.

The lack of praise and validation among educators is so deeply embedded in the culture of schools that it is simply taken for granted; it draws little attention. But having educators live by a norm they would never impose on students is not just a conceptual irony, it is a real-world calamity. It violates the most basic principles of learning and a large body of evidence about how to create and sustain high performance in the workplace. Even worse, the cure, unlike most school improvements, is cheap and straightforward. Most measures that would make a significant difference in school performance are expensive and complex—replacing all our decrepit school buildings, say, or improving all public school teacher-pupil ratios to a genuinely teachable size, or bringing high-quality professional development to every teacher. But dramatically increasing the levels of meaningful recognition for—and among—educators is inexpensive and uncomplicated. It is, I'm convinced, the single best low-cost–high-leverage way to improve morale, performance, the climate for change. In one way or another, virtually every successful school leader I've ever known has been a good "recognizer." There are far too few of them.

The Continuing Recognition Deficit

I once imagined that I could do something to correct the imbalance with respect to recognition. When I first began writing about the subject more than fifteen years ago, I argued that few aspects of American education were more self-defeating than the pitiful levels of acknowledgment and celebration that educators receive and share. I noted that at large educational conferences I would ask audiences how many came from a school or district where there was any kind of formal recognition (even something as nominal as a pin for twenty-five years of service), and that at best, roughly one-third of those attending would raise their hands. They would mention, with little enthusiasm, parties for retiring teachers, breakfasts or lunches provided occasionally by parents. And they would mention, with no enthusiasm, Teacher of the Year awards. A few would cite informal recognition by administrators through personal notes, and occasional visits or communication from former students.

Over the past fifteen years I've continued to ask the same question of my audiences and the results continue to be the same. I have now been in more than twelve hundred schools and have met teachers from several thousand others at conferences. Their accounts continue to confirm the scarcity of recognition in their lives. Long ago I learned to assume that every educator I met had likely gone at least a week and probably a month without receiving—or giving to a colleague—a genuine professional compliment, a piece of specific, performance-related feedback based on personal knowledge and conveying informed appreciation of effort or achievement. To this day I've had no reason to revise this assumption. To be sure, the concept of strengths-based leadership has begun to grow more popular, and I do now occasionally visit a school that has developed a successful way of improving recognition. This is always a delight, but it always stands out as a dramatic exception.

Such malnourishment would not be nearly so problematic if teachers' own work didn't consist of doing for students precisely what teachers don't do for themselves. As I noted in the preceding chapter, one of the fundamental truths about learning is that it is always easier to build on a strength than to attack a weakness. Good teachers certainly help students overcome weaknesses, but they especially help students build on their strengths. They encourage even small signs of progress. Yet the improvement plans most schools make are almost entirely defect based, addressing questions like, What are we doing wrong? What are others doing that we're not? What should we do sooner and faster? They rarely include questions like, What are we doing well and how might we do more of it? There is nothing wrong with asking the first set of questions. There is something very wrong with asking only that set. It flies in the face of what we know about learning.

It also flies in the face of what we know about nourishing performance and growth in the workplace. In the organizational development field, recognition is widely seen as key to workers' job satisfaction, motivation, and performance. As the organizational psychologist Dov Eden, among others, has pointed out, recognition not only strengthens learning, stimulates effort, and raises self-confidence, it leads to better communication and trust and inclines people to raise their own performance expectations.[2] These benefits are particularly important when people are asked to extend themselves, develop new skills, and implement significant change. As we have seen, change threatens competence, relationships, even the meaningfulness of work itself. The more profound and far reaching an innovation, the more anxious it makes people and the more they will need confirmation of the adequacy of their effort and outcomes.

There are many reasons recognition is rare in schools and a focus on the negative is so common. Some are external (rising demands for achievement in the face of diminishing student readiness, a deep, sustained drop in status and in public appreciation and respect for educators); some are historical (education's roots as a calling marked by sacrifice, its history as mostly women's work); others are inherent in the makeup of those who choose classroom careers (a preference for being with their students rather than with other adults); still others are cultural (strong norms of individual autonomy). Collectively, these and other influences present a real challenge to leaders who want to promote and sustain morale, performance, and growth. Actually, four challenges: whether recognition should be intrinsic or extrinsic; how it should be applied; how it can be genuine; and how it can flow laterally among faculty.

Intrinsic Versus Extrinsic

There is a considerable literature about the differences between intrinsic and extrinsic motivators. This literature confirms that the former are almost always the more powerful, especially over a sustained period of time. In fact, emphasizing the latter can be quite counterproductive. This case was made compellingly fifty years ago by Frederick Herzberg, who developed a theory of job satisfaction and motivation that remains useful today. Herzberg drew a distinction between two types of factors that he called *hygienic* and *motivators*.[3] The former relate to the situation in which one works; the latter, to the work one actually does. Hygienic factors are extrinsic to the work itself. They include salary, policy and administration, supervision, working conditions, relationships with peers, and so on. If they are poorly handled they have the potential to be what Herzberg called *dissatisfiers*. If salaries are low, if offices are dirty, if equipment is broken, if the boss plays favorites, staff will be dissatisfied and their performance will suffer. Addressing these shortcomings will reduce people's dissatisfaction and its impact on their performance, but it will not generate lasting satisfaction or stimulate their personal investment in their work. It won't inspire commitment to the organization's basic purpose or encourage extra effort or exceptional performance. For example, raising faculty salaries twenty percent will make people ecstatic—this year. But if the next year's raise is only two percent they'll be disappointed. Similarly, a teacher who hates teaching may reduce his absenteeism if good attendance is tied to higher pay, but he will not love teaching more or involve himself more fervently in school improvement.

Herzberg's model helps explain why merit pay plans, contrary to the stubborn beliefs of many businesspeople who serve on school boards, are poor vehicles for recognizing and stimulating teacher performance and have such a truly dismal track record. It's not just that most plans offer stipends that are too few and too small to be appealing, or that teachers see the awarding of the "merit" bonuses as arbitrary and simplistic. (Anyone who has ever taught knows that you often do your best work with a class that underperforms—precisely because it is so difficult to teach.) Nor is it just that teachers have little thirst for outpointing colleagues. It's that teachers do not become teachers for the money (only a fool would!). They want to be adequately compensated, and they can be dissatisfied, in Herzberg's terms, by being grossly underpaid, but they are simply not driven by compensation in the way that corporate professionals often seem to be. Given all this, merit pay plans not only fail to make teachers feel adequately recognized, they frequently provoke cynicism and hostility. They are a textbook example of how an emphasis on extrinsic rewards can actually hamper a school's ability to promote growth in its staff and thus improve its performance.

To raise the ceiling rather than just reinforce the floor, I have argued that one must attend to the motivators, or *satisfiers*, as Herzberg also called them. These are characteristics intrinsic to one's job, such as the nature of the work itself, responsibility, achievement, advancement—and, notably, recognition.[4] In education, studies dating back several decades have confirmed that intrinsic rewards such as having exciting work, seeing students achieve, and fulfilling competently a task one views as important, are consistently more powerful engines of performance than salary.[5] Acknowledging and thanking people for fulfilling worthy goals and noble purposes helps to reinforce the school's basic values and vision. It is here that real potential for improvement lies.

Wide and Deep

Given that levels of intrinsic recognition must be raised, the second key question is what is the best way to do this? Is it better to recognize people individually or in groups, formally or informally, privately or publicly? For me, the answer to all these questions has always been, Yes. The core principle of recognition is to apply it wherever possible. Savvy leaders tend to be natural reinforcers and validaters. They tend to be enthusiastic, both about their goals and the potential of people to fulfill them. They are not necessarily flamboyant, although some are. Many of the best do lots of modeling and encouraging, noticing and asking, approving and supporting. In one way or another, however, good leaders are on the lookout for evidence of effort and improvement and express their appreciation when they see either—even in small increments. It has long seemed to me that school improvement is too often approached on an all-or-nothing basis, especially by those who see themselves as hard-nosed about accountability. They want educators to undertake a change *and* achieve it before offering recognition. To return briefly to Perverse Academy, this would be analogous to telling students on the first day of school, "I will tolerate no mistakes. You will answer every question correctly the very first time." What better way to cripple learning than to take away the freedom to err? Doing so misunderstands not only human nature but the nature of new learning, which requires that people do *more* and *different* first and then start to do *better*.

When school leaders are seeking improvement they need to remember that this begins with getting people to try something new or to try the same thing harder. To build momentum, one must start by rewarding interest, curiosity, exploration. Savvy leaders especially attend to the last. Particularly in the early going, when uncertainty is highest, they acknowledge *any* kind of experimentation with new practices. They try to affirm teachers' effort as well as success, however modest. In time, of course, they expect to see genuine improvement in results. Even then, it is often wise to employ what Dov Eden calls "a strategy of small wins," in which the leader defines a major innovation in terms of a series of smaller stages and builds momentum "by encouraging participants to savor the joys of successive small accomplishments that signal milestones along the way toward achieving more ambitious goals."[6]

A cornerstone of this approach is to make it safe to try. Again, this is what teachers at Perverse Academy would not do, and it is a basic condition for human learning. It is vital to avoid penalizing those who try but don't succeed at first. The "excellence" literature of the 1980s had many flaws, but one of its strengths was that it was replete with examples of America's top corporations' rewarding their people for trying innovations, even when these didn't initially succeed. Companies that invest in research and development and those that depend on staff creativity usually provide all sorts of inducements to encourage people to propose and try new initiatives, and they accept the inevitable "error rate" that comes with experimentation. They know that the perfect is the enemy of the good. If we truly want schools to become learning organizations, their leaders—and the people to whom their leaders answer—need to avoid perfectionism, to see some level of error as inevitable in an endeavor as complex as schooling; to see it, in fact, the way good teachers do when working with students, as an opportunity for growth.

Implicit in this approach to recognition is the importance of managing expectations. This is a key way in which leaders influence staff. As we saw in Chapter Four, people don't react to the events themselves but to what these events mean. Meaning is shaped by many things, chief among them the leader's definition. Whether a mistake is just a slip-up or a proof of utter incompetence or an opportunity for learning often depends on how the leader defines it. One way leaders use recognition effectively is by *reframing*, which means redefining a concept, behavior, event, or relationship by situating it in a different context, approaching it from a different angle. Reframing can give people a new perspective, helping them broaden and modify the patterns by which they understand the world.

Reframing can be as simple as helping people see that a glass is half full rather than half empty, or, when the glass is less than half full, that it is as full as it can currently be. I still recall the example of a principal I'll call Jane Green, whom I met long ago, halfway through her first year at an impoverished, low-performing urban elementary school. "What has surprised me most," she told me, "is not how bad this school is, but how good it is, *given what it's up against.*" In one sentence, she began to recast the school's entire situation. She didn't deny its own weaknesses, but she saw them in light of larger challenges the school faced and conditions it couldn't control. Ever since, when I visit a "bad" school that serves impoverished children, I remember her words.

When a leader like Jane Green reframes a situation she doesn't demand that people change the way they understand events, but she offers them a new way to do so. She enables them to enlarge their framework for understanding. Doing so validates for people the reality of the challenges facing them. This is often deeply comforting and encouraging, especially when the obstacles seem intractable and progress is slow. In psychology we refer to this kind of reframing as "normalizing" because it helps people to see that a particular challenge is not unique to them and that their failure to master it is expectable, or at least understandable, not proof of their inadequacy. When provided by a leader who is respected, this kind of intervention can exert a powerful positive impact on staff morale and energy. It makes it easier for everyone to buy into a strategy of small wins and to keep trying.

Sincerely, Specifically Yours

None of this means being disingenuous. As vital as it is—indeed, precisely because it is so vital—recognition can't be false or forced. If it is, the effort will backfire, damaging the leader's credibility and the faculty's morale. The first requirement for success is sincerity. When leaders praise or acknowledge, they have to mean it—at least most of the time. Reframing is not a panacea; trying to recast all failures and disappointments in a positive light is self-defeating. Ernest Hemingway famously said that a writer must have "a built-in, shock-proof, crap detector." We're not all Hemingways, but most of us can sense it when someone with whom we frequently interact is insincere. Groucho Marx wasn't replying to Hemingway but could have been when he said, "Sincerity is everything—if you can fake that, you've got it made." All leaders have to do some faking, such as lauding a retiring teacher whose departure is long overdue, for example. Most of us cut them some slack in such situations. But when a leader is consistently or regularly disingenuous it destroys our trust and respect.

The obvious kind of insincerity is found in leaders who are calculating and manipulative, who seem to be out for themselves rather than genuinely interested in others. In my experience, they are rare in schools, but once their habit of insincerity becomes clear they arouse suspicion whenever they praise and acknowledge people. Less malignant but much more common are leaders who are well meaning and positive but who flood their teachers with bland, generic compliments. They're not devious or deceitful, but they're not authentic, either. They strike faculty as naïve or out of it; it's hard to take their compliments seriously. Though very different from the Machiavellian types, they, too are soon discounted.

The way to make sure that recognition is effective is to make sure it is authentic, which requires that it be specific. When a superintendent or principal or school head gives specific examples of specific people doing specific things or grappling with specific challenges, people know she *knows*. This is true whether she is speaking individually to one teacher or addressing the whole faculty. Many school leaders, for instance, send out a weekly staff memo. The most effective are not always the best prose stylists but the ones who can capture particular events—an interchange they saw in a class or a comment a student made about a teacher—and connect these to the larger purposes of the school.

If sincerity is a necessity then recognition must be earned; there has to be something worth recognizing. But if praise is not to be false and reframing is not a panacea, what about goals that aren't met, projects and programs that take too long or come up short? When achievement can't be praised, one must try to acknowledge effort and validate challenge. Jane Green proved to be adept at this. She knew that the changes she began requiring of her teachers—new curriculum, new methods, more collaboration, and so on—would be difficult for many. She focussed on evidence of effort and acknowledged it (with specifics) wherever she saw it. She listened respectfully to staff concerns about what she was asking of them, made adjustments where she could, but was candid about where she couldn't and confirmed clearly that she understood the challenge this posed. Every now and then, she admitted, she had to fake the sincerity a bit. But for the most part, her praise and acknowledgment were genuine. Even teachers who were strongly opposed to her agenda found her recognition meaningful.

Lateral

There remains one key challenge about recognition: how to help it flow laterally among faculty. What recognition one can find in schools almost always runs from the top down, from the head or principal. This inevitably limits what teachers receive. It also leaves them in a dependent position and absolves them of collegial responsibility. If they are to thrive and grow, praise, acknowledgment, and validation must be regular features of their own give-and-take at school.

The issue here is not that schools aren't positive places or that educators don't respond well to one another. Far from it. Most schools tend to be full of nice people who are cordial to and supportive of one another. They cover classes and study halls for one another. If asked, they offer advice about a student or a lesson. If one suffers an illness or has a family crisis the rest rally to help. This is all to the good. What they don't provide for one another is meaningful recognition concerning the work of schooling itself. Most schools are, as Roland Barth has pointed out, *congenial* but not *collegial*.[7] Congeniality is about getting along well, being friendly and warm, and so on. Collegiality is a step beyond. It is about promoting professional growth through collaboration: actively learning from one another by discussing practice, observing one another's teaching, planning jointly, and the like. Its focus is development, not sociability. Congeniality is vital: a school without it is an unhappy place to work; it is the platform on which collegiality is built. But by itself it does not provide adequate professional recognition. Collegiality involves more than just recognition—among other things, a truly collegial faculty is one that has learned how to disagree candidly and constructively— but collegiality provides an ideal conduit for recognition.

Despite the apparent value of moving beyond congeniality, school leaders who decide to do so and to raise recognition levels often run into resistance on the part of teachers, a phenomenon I have explored in more depth in *The Human Side of School Change*. Here I will just note that although we have to assume that their brains are wired like everyone else's and hence crave acknowledgment and appreciation, educators can be quite ambivalent about being recognized, especially publicly. It makes many uncomfortable and some much more than uncomfortable. I have always thought it best for the leader to tackle this reluctance straight on, making it a formal focus of faculty discussion. The leader can challenge teachers to address the double standard, point out the damage that would be done to student learning by the PA Way, make clear that his goal is not to single out some teachers at the expense of others but "to celebrate together examples of us at our best," and to emphasize the importance of finding meaningful, not artificial ways of doing this.

Teachers typically advance a number of reasons why this effort won't work. One of the first is that they have no real basis for offering one another genuine recognition because they know so little about their colleagues' actual practice. They form impressions from hearing them talk at meetings, hearing what students say about them, and so on, but rarely have much firsthand knowledge. This objection opens the door to larger and potentially fruitful discussions about how to promote genuine collegiality. In a number of schools where I have worked, it has led to such steps as organized peer observations: teachers pair up and take turns watching each other teach and they debrief afterward. In some schools this approach is expanded and institutionalized through critical friends groups and professional learning communities. But even in severely demoralized schools, I have seen a single round of visits make a material improvement in recognition and morale and spark, here and there, a new focus on practice.

In addition to these kinds of steps there are many small, no-cost ways to improve recognition. An elementary school can rotate faculty meetings among teachers' classrooms. The host teacher briefly introduces the room's layout and materials and explains why she's arranged them as she has. There is nothing formal or lengthy, but it offers a quick chance for people to learn about—and acknowledge—one another's work. Any school can begin faculty meetings with a brief opportunity—no obligation—for people to acknowledge colleagues for certain aspects of their work. It doesn't particularly matter what a faculty adopts as a recognition vehicle, so long as it is meaningful to all concerned. It can be formal, substantive, and serious, or informal, symbolic, and light. In my experience the latter is much more common. At a conference years ago a middle school teacher described the "Golden Plunger Award" her school had created: a toilet plunger, spray-painted gold, which a teacher could present to a colleague at a faculty meeting if the donor knew the recipient had tried something new in her class and it had bombed. The recipient would have to stand, accept the plunger, and recount the "failure," which would be greeted with great applause. "We have fun with it," she said, "there's never anything malicious. And it really helps keep it safe to try, to keep trying, and to not have to be perfect."

A Help, Not a Cure

At its best, an emphasis on recognition is an ideal antidote to the PA Way, but it is not a complete solution. There will inevitably be times when the leader has to apply pressure first and offer recognition later, or at least temper the provision of recognition with pressure, as did the new head of an independent secondary school who told me that he found the faculty much more self-satisfied than they deserved to be. "We're seen as a 'high-performing' school," he said, "but we're actually taking lots of credit for outputs that mostly reflect inputs. We have the most teachable kids in America and they're in very small classes. We could be doing much more with them." Individually, his teachers were engaged in their own teaching, "but they are not focussed on professional growth. They're not really challenging themselves or the students." His concern could be applied to more than a few schools that serve very advantaged students.

In schools like this, just as in the lowest-performing schools, there is work to be done, some of it hard and unpleasant. But even—especially—in the schools that need the most change, recognition will eventually play an important part in encouraging and then sustaining movement in the right direction. A leader who needs a faculty to confront its shortcomings and raise its game will have a much easier time if he optimizes recognition, both top-down and lateral. The behaviors and habits that lead to progress and to exemplary performance can't simply be demanded; they have to be fostered. Savvy leaders know that no school can flourish unless everyone in it, not just its students, is well nourished.

Chapter Seven

The Seventh Secret

From Savvy to Wise: Look Out for Number One

It's got to be the going, not the getting there that's good.

—Harry Chapin[1]

I BEGAN THIS BOOK BY NOTING THAT MANY SCHOOL LEADERS, although they love education, find that their jobs are, if not eating them up, eating into their lives, posing both professional questions—Can I do it all? Can I master all that is asked of me?—and personal questions—What does it take out of me to do it all? What about the rest of my life? The preceding chapters have explored ways that savvy leaders tackle the professional challenge, the outlook and inclinations they bring to bear, specific steps they take. As we have seen, they accept inevitabilities (the dilemmas of leadership, the resistance to change, the rising tide of unrealistic expectations) and adjust their behavior and goals accordingly, but they also assert their competence and priorities (leading from strength, clarifying their core commitments, fostering recognition), thus bringing focus and concentration to their work. All this makes leadership more doable and increases the chances of doing it well. And it brings another signal advantage: it makes a personal life possible.

Possible, but not inevitable. The savvy school leaders I meet are all hard workers who are committed to their calling and find it a source of meaning and fulfillment. But a good number acknowledge that they shortchange personal and family life. Their mastery of the previous six secrets enables them to excel professionally but doesn't guarantee balance between work and other pursuits. A smaller number are not just savvy but wise. They have mastered the seventh secret: they have learned to look out for themselves. They don't let their jobs devour them or they recognize it when it starts to happen and extricate themselves. They apply to themselves what I think of as the Oxygen Mask Rule, which every air traveler hears before take off ("In the event of a loss of cabin pressure . . . put on your own mask first, then help others around you"). They've learned that you must take care of yourself so that you can take care of others, that if you only give to others without giving to yourself you will eventually give out. Being appropriately self-centered and looking out for Number One not only enriches their personal lives and family relationships, it improves their leadership. What it requires is, like so much else in this book, simple but not easy: making choices, modifying expectations, and indulging oneself, all of which—including the last—lead to wisdom.

Balance Requires Choice

Overwork is prevalent in professional circles across America. Jobs consume ever more of our time and energy, shrinking our ability to be at home and our engagement when we are.

This phenomenon has become a field of study, *work-life balance*, and boasts a literature of several thousand books and articles and an array of foundations, companies, and consultants all deploring work-life *im*balance and pursuing its causes and cure. Although the language of overwork and imbalance tends to emphasize victimization (unfeeling, productivity-driven employers; vulnerable, ill-treated workers), the picture is more complex. Many professionals, it turns out, are complicit in their own overwork. For them, career has become a form of self-expression, a primary source of meaning. Some fields offer opportunities to tackle exciting, challenging, cutting-edge projects, often with the potential for great financial reward and the cachet that comes with being a ground-breaking entrepreneur. Many professionals complain about how much they work, yet keep investing themselves in their jobs.

School leaders are hardly the only ones on this list, but in my experience they are prominently represented. They ignore the Oxygen Mask Rule in droves. For many of those I meet, the lure of work includes a sense of high mission: the apparently urgent need to transform our schools, close the achievement gap, prepare workers who will keep America atop the global economy, and knit together our heterogeneous social fabric. A heavy burden? Certainly, but also a source of satisfaction. The two are inseparable, as William James pointed out over a century ago: "Everything added to the Self is a burden [and] a pride."[2] Most school administrators I meet feel that they have almost no way to control or reduce the growing demands of their jobs. What they don't realize, or don't acknowledge, is that they have actually chosen many of their burdens and accepted, even embraced, others that have been imposed on them.

James caught the burden-pride dilemma perfectly. He knew that the characteristics, commitments, and responsibilities in which we take pride are often onerous. Good leaders, for example, are typically good problem solvers and enjoy the feeling of being effective and exercising power and the status this brings them. "I like being the go-to guy," as a superintendent says. Of course, being an effective go-to problem solver only encourages more people with problems to seek him out. Good leaders also know it makes a positive difference if they attend the funerals and weddings of staff members' family members, even though doing so requires foregoing time with their own families. Fulfilling these kinds of roles is, well, fulfilling. It confirms the leader's importance but also his sense of being responsible, of taking good care of his people.

This conscientiousness turns out to be a slippery slope. Over time, effective leaders tend to grow ever more invested in their professional roles, to identify themselves ever more closely with the institution. They start saying "my school," for instance, instead of "our school." They skip their own children's Little League games to attend sports contests at their school. They call in to the secretary daily while on vacation. They interrupt their summer travel to interview replacements for staff who announce sudden departures. ("I'm like Don Corleone in *The Godfather*," says a principal. "I insist on hearing bad news at once." He presents it as a weight he must bear, but there is a clear hint of pride in the comparison he chooses.) Leaders complain about these responsibilities, even as they embrace more of them, protesting that they have no choice ("If I don't do it, who will?"). They even take a perverse pride in menial management burdens, such as making sure that red tape requirements are met or that custodians keep the bathrooms clean. "Amazing, isn't it?" says a headmaster. "I shouldn't have to do this stuff." But he does it, and over time, as he admits, he has come to be proud of his capacity to bear these burdens, even though he resents them. Like other devoted leaders, he is the architect of his overwork, not just its prisoner.

Whatever its roots and rewards, overwork comes at a price. To many pediatricians, psychologists, teachers, and others who work with children, one of the chief casualties of the resulting imbalance is parenting. As we have seen, educators everywhere complain that parents spend too little time with their children, fail to teach them essential lessons about life, try to hurry their growing up, and then atone for the ensuing guilt by overindulging and overprotecting them. Although school leaders are hardly the only executives to overwork, they often feel particularly conflicted about engaging in the very behavior they and their teachers criticize. Some resolve to do less paperwork on weekends, others try to sneak in weekend paperwork so as to be freer during the week. Some try to come home earlier after school (bringing paperwork to do in the evening), others stay later at school doing paperwork so as to be "really free" when they do get home. Underneath these and other efforts lies, unspoken, a futile assumption: "If I can just be more efficient and manage my time at work better, I can get everything done and have more time for self and family." This is the Efficiency Fantasy. It will never be fulfilled. The truth, as Robert Reich learned, is stark and simple: balance requires choice.

Among the many things he has done during an engaged and apparently engaging life, Reich served as secretary of labor under President Bill Clinton. He loved the job, but he left it because he couldn't find a work-life balance. Balance, to him, meant "doing more of what you really want to do and less of what you don't," but he found this impossible. He loved his family *and* his job and wanted more of both, which was, of course, impossible: he was always shortchanging one or the other. Standard time management methods proved futile. For one thing, the needs and crises of children and spouses can't be scheduled and meaningful routines can't be truncated (think, for example, of the bedtime rituals so precious to toddlers). For another, there is no way to control the timing of opportunities and crises at work—something every school leader knows. Time, as Reich discovered, is the mother of all zero-sum games: hours spent doing one thing in one place are hours not spent doing something else in another. Time insists on choice.[3]

I'm not equating the pressures of being a school leader with those of being a federal cabinet secretary and I'm certainly not arguing that all who want a decent home life should quit their jobs. I cite Reich's example because of his willingness to come to grips with a dilemma most of us fudge—he acknowledged his own personal contribution to his overwork and faced the hard reality that he couldn't have it all, a full work life and a full family life. He had to make choices. Practiced on a smaller scale, his is an ideal way to limit the stresses of leadership and restore balance to one's life.

Coping begins by realizing that time management does not just mean "finding ways to be more efficient so I can do more of the job." This can improve performance and productivity, but it involves a limited notion of choice, and it is not a formula for improving one's well-being or the balance in one's life. The principal I described in Chapter Five, who ignored the paperwork from the central office, enabled herself to concentrate on her own priorities as principal, but wasn't improving her work-life balance. To achieve that, time management must mean "I will be as efficient as I can reasonably be within limits that create space for the other important things in my life." It can't mean, "I will be all things to all people all the time." As Lisa Darling, a savvy, successful independent school head, says, "Leading a school is the most extraordinarily privileged and important work I can imagine doing—and at the same time, it's just a job. Staying clear about both facets is what has kept me reasonably sane over the years!"[4] Balance, that is, involves not just making choices *at* work regarding which tasks deserve priority and which can be delegated, but making choices *about* work, about how much of oneself will be invested in the work itself.

There is no single correct balance. Some leaders, for example, are single or no longer raising children at home and have fewer family demands; they can be freer to engage at school. Others, no matter what their family status, simply find work especially rewarding. But for those who wish to limit overwork, Reich's lesson is essential. Ever since I read his article, whenever I meet effective school leaders who do not radiate a sense of being highly stressed and who succeed without sacrificing everything to their work, I ask how they manage this. Without exception, they, like Lisa Darling, report having explicitly chosen to seek balance and having translated this commitment into rules or guidelines that focus and limit their work. Here are examples of what some of them do:

- An elementary principal has his secretary handle all phone calls, mail, and e-mail. He never does school e-mail from home. ("It took a while, but people got used to not hearing back from me that evening or over the weekend," he says. "If there's a real crisis, they call me.")

- A superintendent's daily schedule specifies both her arrival time in the morning *and* her departure time in the afternoon. Her secretary is primed to remind her of the latter, if necessary.

- When he was hired, a high school principal whose own children are in middle school made it an explicit condition of accepting the job that he would not attend every athletic contest, play performance, and dance. (When, during his first year, the mother of a varsity athlete asked him why he missed some games, he replied—nicely—"While I would be watching your son play, who would be watching mine?")

- A middle school principal's schedule designates specific times each week for classroom visits and being "out and about the school," for "interruptible" office work (his door is open), and for "non-interruptible" office work (his door is closed; he is off-limits "unless a student is bleeding").

- Twice each year an elementary principal must devote an entire day to writing teacher evaluations.

She does so on a weekday, not a weekend, and from home.

- An independent school head and his wife have a regularly scheduled biweekly "date night."

These choices are small, but not insignificant. And they are not the only things each of these leaders does to avoid overwork. The results aren't perfect. None of these educators claims to live a stress-free, perfectly balanced life. All make exceptions to their rules as conditions require, but not too many exceptions. To a person, they believe they function better at work because they control its hold on them. And thanks to these and other choices they make, each enjoys a better quality of life than their workaholic peers. They feel less guilty, too. "I work hard," says a principal, "and I expect my teachers to work hard. But we have too much workaholism among the parents in my school. I don't model that and I don't want my teachers modeling that."

The Bruno Lesson: Reach and Realism

Setting limits on one's time at work means accepting limits on what one expects to achieve. It doesn't mean taking it easy or settling for mediocre performance, it means doing over a sustained period of time everything one reasonably can but not imagining that one can heal the sick and raise the dead. The dilemmas facing schools and those built into leadership all call for moderating expectations. They don't call for giving up on goals and standards, but for working hard and measuring progress fully and fairly—that is, assessing where we are, not just in terms of where we wish to get but also in terms of where we started and the constraints upon us. This is a combination I have always thought of as *reach and realism*. My most powerful lesson in it came decades ago in my second year of teaching.

I was an English teacher at an excellent suburban Boston high school where most students went on to college. But I and other young faculty grew interested in the lowest-performing students. They were mostly boys, mostly poor readers, and not headed for college. They took all their courses in the "Basic" (bottom-level) track, where the English I course emphasized grammar and bored them to death. We convinced our superintendent to let us create a new English I and to reduce class sizes (from twenty-five to fifteen). A team of us labored all summer to write a full year of lesson plans that we hoped would excite students and make them want to read, write, and think. Our lessons certainly excited us. September found me full of anticipation: three of my five sections were to be in English I. I couldn't wait. I had no idea that disaster loomed.

One of my English I sections met last period. It immediately disintegrated, thanks to a big, burly, loudmouthed boy I'll call Jim Curley, who began eating me alive. Day after day he'd arrive late and dismantle my lesson. He wasn't mean or nasty, he was a motormouth, a comedian. He fidgeted and twitched. He hummed to himself. He couldn't stay in his seat or keep his hands off other students. He blurted out deliberately wrong answers, bad jokes, and puns—endless, horrible puns. Today he would surely be seen as having ADHD; back then he was just a royal pain. Nothing I tried, whether I reached out to him or got tough with him, worked for more than a day or so. He was single-handedly trashing my dream of transforming education for our neediest students, as well as my view of myself as a teacher who could connect with them. Some days I'd go home with a splitting headache and take a nap. I was only twenty-four, but I'd nap. By Thanksgiving I was scanning the absence list each morning, hoping—guiltily—to find Jim's name. If it wasn't there I'd start dreading the prospect of last period.

In desperation I turned to a colleague, Don Thomas, the epitome of a savvy educator. To this day I've met few smarter people. He taught ingenious lessons in semiotics to students of all levels. And he was utterly self-possessed. I begged him to help me. He agreed to teach a lesson while I watched. When the day arrived, I introduced him and sat in the back of the room. Several minutes later, Jim barged in and, seeing a new teacher, stood in the doorway, doing a long, exaggerated double-take to register his surprise. I waited to see the master in action; Don ignored him. This surprised Jim, who eventually sat down. He was briefly quiet, then began bits of his routine—nudging the boy on one side of him, winking at the girl on the other, staring ostentatiously out the window. Don ignored these. Jim accelerated his pace, making a few sotto voce wisecracks. These, too, Don ignored. Finally, as Jim reached full flower, whistling and grimacing at another student's answer, Don frowned across the small circle, as if he had just now discovered Jim, and barked in a loud, deep voice, "Hey, Bruno, shut up!"

Everyone was stunned—no one more than I. That's all Don said to Jim. He never tried to engage him in the lesson. No feeding him straight lines ("What do you think about that idea, Jim?") as I had been doing, which just set up his jokes. Don showed him up and then hung him out to dry. Confronted by a no-nonsense stranger with a powerful presence, deprived of a foil, Jim stayed under moderate control.

At the end of the class Don said two things to me. The first was unforgettable—unforgettable because it was not merely unhelpful, it was unbelievable. He said matter-of-factly, "I took the kid by surprise. That'll never work again; don't try that." (As though tomorrow I might summon my full authority as a young, second-year teacher and say, "Hey, Bruno, shut up!") But the second thing he said was life altering. He asked me how many minutes a day I expected Jim to pay attention. "Fifty," I said, "that's the class." Don shook his head. "A kid like this," he said, "you'd be lucky to get *ten* minutes of attention and luckier still if they were *consecutive*." Think about it: an adolescent male who can't read, has ADHD but no medication, in an English class at 3:00 in the afternoon. If you're the teacher, this is unfair to you. Much more important, if you're the student, this is unfair to you. Jim had needs I knew nothing about meeting.

Things were never great that year—Jim didn't have a miraculous turnaround; I was guiltily glad any time he was out sick—but they were never as awful again, and the reason was that I now had two standards in my head: fifty minutes and ten: my full goal and the true baseline. I never gave up wanting fifty minutes and I never got it, but I could see that when we got to fifteen we were up five. I stopped discounting slow and small progress. I focussed less on what Jim couldn't do and more on what he (and hence what I) could do. Reinforcing the successes generated more of them. In retrospect, given Jim's condition, my inexperience, and the lack of knowledge about ADHD in those days, the rest of the year was about the best it could be.

Don's lesson has stayed with me ever since. A key to success for everyone at every level in a school is to balance reach (high strivings) against realism (the full context of factors that affect performance), to measure progress *up against* a meaningful goal and *up from* the beginning baseline, and to remember that the latter is always the truer gauge of progress. Good teachers don't abandon their high standards but they don't ignore what constitute real gains for their students. Good leaders adopt the same approach to their schools. As we have seen, teachers rarely apply the same approach to themselves or their colleagues; they need a good leader to help them do this. Good leaders, for their part, need to guard against the same blind spot. Just as teachers need to do for themselves what they do for students, leaders need to do for themselves what they do for teachers.

The Uses of Self-Indulgence

The difficulty, of course, is that leaders have no one immediately at hand to help them, no one with the purchase and the standing to do for them what they do for teachers. Although they might theoretically be able to incorporate the Bruno Lesson through sheer willpower (forcing themselves to repeat "reach and realism" every morning, perhaps), three practical steps are helpful, steps of the kind that the wisest leaders take. Each involves a measure of self-indulgence: get support, drink cognac, lighten up.

The first step couldn't be more obvious. Everything we know about stress confirms that it is exacerbated by isolation and reduced by support. In making the case for leaders' providing recognition and fostering its spread among staff, Chapter Six made no mention of leaders' *receiving* recognition. The reason? It so rarely happens. Recognition, like water, rarely flows uphill very long. How could it be otherwise, given that so much of what leaders do is unseen by—and often unexplainable to—teachers, parents, and the community? Because, as Chapter Two argued, isolation is so embedded in leadership, it is vital to connect with others.

Leaders need to seek out occasions when they can gather as peers to share their own recognition, acknowledgment, and feedback. An excellent way to do this is to go away—to attend conferences and conventions, preferably those held in agreeable settings with comfortable accommodations. For years I have teased principals and especially superintendents and independent school heads about going on boondoggles and junkets—events that offer, under the cover of professional development, a chance to get away, often with one's spouse, and connect with one's peers. I am often asked to help provide the cover, that is, to speak at these conferences. When I first started doing this, I imagined that the lectures and workshops were *the* point of the events, but I soon learned that they were *a* point. There is inevitably an inspirational theme emblazoned on the program books, tote bags, and name tags given to participants ("Creating Tomorrow's Schools," "Forging Our Children's Future," and the like), but at most meetings an equally accurate title would be something like, "Schmoozing with My Pals and Peers." I say this with no hint of disrespect. The schmoozing makes a material difference to leaders' performance and well-being. As I've already noted, it is mainly at conferences and conventions that leaders can gather with the only peers they have, that they can compare notes, share anecdotes and frustrations, gossip, rediscover that the challenges facing them are not unique, and troubleshoot common dilemmas. At the best meetings, they leave stimulated and better informed thanks to the speakers, and with their perspective restored, their energy renewed, their priorities reinforced, and feeling less alone—all thanks to one another.

Ideally, one shouldn't have to travel to get support; there should be local options. One of these is job-alike support groups. For almost twenty years one of the best parts of my professional life has been the second Thursday of each month, which is when a group of elementary principals meets at my house. Our membership has changed over the years, but our conversation still ranges from the deadly serious to the wildly humorous and from high philosophy to carpool dismissal dilemmas. Members get and give useful advice, a larger context, sympathy, and praise and acknowledgment (that is, actual, genuine recognition). In some school districts administrators hold similar meetings. These are not agenda-driven or task-oriented, but aimed specifically at connection and support. Given the pressures on schools it can be hard to schedule these meetings frequently enough and to keep the normal business out of them, but where they work well and become institutionalized they improve administrators' decision making and their well-being.

The second step is less obvious but equally important: leaders should acquire a taste for expensive French cognac. The definition of this substance is easy: it comes from France, its minimum price is fifty dollars per bottle, and somewhere on its label are the letters "V.S.O.P." or "X.O." It should be drunk from a fine-quality snifter, not a juice glass. It is the ideal vehicle to encourage the taking of perspective. If you acquire this taste you can do as my wife and I do. On some Friday nights about nine o'clock, which is just when we used to be going out and is now just as we're getting ready for bed (everyone can go out on Saturday, but only the young go out on Friday, too), we pour small snifters of this expensive spirit and for a few moments we indulge ourselves. I'm as pretentious as I wish. I swirl the cognac in the glass, I inhale its *bouquet*, and I imagine what I damn please. I imagine, for example, that when people find out I'm a psychologist, they don't instantly assume that my own children must be screwed up. I imagine that the staff at my clinic appreciate everything that I do for them, it's just that they haven't mentioned it lately. You can imagine anything you want and you can omit the alcohol. If you don't like it, if you have a bad drinking history, if you have religious principles that forbid it, leave it out. What you need is a *cognac factor*.

A cognac factor is a treat you give yourself. When you take this treat you step outside yourself, you look back in, and you give yourself recognition for two things. First, you take credit for what you have done, instead of dwelling on what you haven't. If you began the week with eight major items on your to-do list, completed three and added one, you think about the three. Second, you take credit not for how well you've done but for being willing to do it. Are your burdens a source of pride? They ought to be, at least some of them. What mission could be nobler, what calling more important than education? Those who make a sacrifice to educate the young are doing what anyone should see as God's work. It deserves to be celebrated as such.

The third step flows directly from the second. A cognac factor will help you do what the wisest leaders do: lighten up. Intense perfectionism and failure-is-not-an-option heroism may produce remarkable results, but only briefly or intermittently. Eventually—sooner rather than later, in most cases—they lead to self-absorption and then burnout. The best leaders work very hard but not without letup. They take their work very seriously, but not themselves. They know how to laugh. Fortunately, schools are full of children and adolescents, so there is plenty to laugh about. Here are two examples I treasure.

Mike Babcock was the much-loved, highly respected head of the Polytechnic School in Pasadena, California, a school he attended as a student and served first as a teacher and then, for eighteen years, as its leader. Mike is a savvy, sincere, generous, thoughtful educator who cares deeply about whether a school is a good place for students and a good place for teachers. He's also bald, which is important to this story he tells:

> I was walking next to the primary play yard. Two kinder-gartners were playing in the sand, and as I came by they greeted me. One of them said, "I know who you are." When I asked who, he replied, "You're the headmaster." And without a pause, the other lad said, "Yeah, and if you had any hair, you could be the hairmaster."[5]

Moments like this are priceless. Those who work in elementary schools get lots of them. In high schools there are not as many, but there are still plenty. I happened upon one in a large urban high school in the northeast. It was late May, the weather had been hot and muggy for a week, and the ancient, decrepit building had no air conditioning and poor ventilation. The atmosphere was oppressive. The girls had started to disrobe, and they had begun from a low baseline. Shortly before I entered, one had been sent out of class for being underdressed. She was wearing two pieces that were surely larger than what she wore to the beach, but much smaller than any normal school attire. She was tall, buxom, and enraged, stomping around the front hall, shouting, surrounded by the principal, an assistant principal, and a security guard, two of them men, trying to corral her without touching her, which was not easy. "The teacher said this was *revealing*," she bellowed, pronouncing the word with venomous scorn. "*Revealing*. I ask you, is this *revealing*?" "You're damn right it is!" I thought to myself. "Extremely revealing—and why weren't they dressed like that when I was in high school?" The situation wasn't mine to resolve. I could smile at it. And so (from a later vantage point) could the principal, the assistant principal, and the security guard.

Lighten-up moments cause laughter and release tension because they confront us directly with truths we minimize or deny. Like peer support and a cognac factor, they lend perspective. All three help us take the measure of things as they truly are and in full context. They bring us back from lofty abstractions of educational theory and grand schemes for school improvement to the reality of working with flesh-and-blood students. They help us validate the burdens and celebrate the prides of schooling and leadership. I don't think it's an exaggeration to call this wisdom. Wisdom in all its meanings: deep insight, common sense, and ancient lore.

The Journey

The ancient lore of many cultures includes tales of heroes who undertake great journeys to reach a destination and who ultimately realize that life is not about reaching the goal, but about making the journey, that indeed life itself is a journey. This is as old—and as relevant—a truth as there is, revisited by every generation. As T. S. Eliot wrote:

> We shall not cease from exploration
> And the end of all our exploring
> Will be to arrive where we started
> And know the place for the first time.[6]

Or, as Henry Miller put it, "one's destination is never a place but rather a new way of looking at things."[7] In its own homey way, this is the lesson that Dorothy learns in *The Wizard of Oz*. It is nowhere more applicable than in schools.

The best schools want to be generative, to instill in students a lifelong love of learning. They want students not just to acquire the three R's and facts, formulas, and concepts but to have a thirst for learning and to learn how to learn so that they can continue to grow and adapt throughout their lives. And ultimately, they want their students to be not just knowledgeable but wise, which requires a capacity to tolerate and learn from error and loss. These broader interests and higher skills, this deeper capacity, develop chiefly through the relationship between teachers and students. They are transmitted through the extended process of their engagement over the years. Think about your own schooling. What stands out about it? This is a question I often ask school board members when I work with them. Their assessment almost always depends primarily on the relationships they had with their teachers, and they always—always—speak about the journey, not the destination.

American education, alas, is currently obsessed with destinations—outcomes too often assessed narrowly by test scores and college admissions. This obsession contributes heavily to the stress felt by school leaders. Its immediate flaw lies in the crudeness and unfairness of the measures, but its deeper defect lies in obscuring the primacy of the journey students make with their teachers. It's not that goals are unimportant or unhelpful: it takes a worthy destination to motivate a journey and to help gauge progress along the way. But the wisest leaders, when they make choices to achieve balance in their lives, when they combine reach and realism, when they seek and offer support, find a cognac factor, and lighten up—when they do these things they're not giving up or being irresponsible. They're acknowledging that their own lives are more than just their work, noble though it is, and that their lives, including their work, are journeys—works in progress—and that so too are the lives of their teachers and students. They're in touch with the deeper meaning and larger purpose of education. And they're empowering themselves to keep doing their very best for all those in their care.

Endnotes

1. When You Go to See the Wizard, Take Toto

1. Paul, 2004.
2. Vaill, 1989, 77.
3. Bennis, 1989, 22–23.
4. Bennis and Nanus, 1985, 4–5.
5. Stewart, 2006, 84.
6. Collins, 2001, 15.
7. Resnick and Smunt, 2004, 6–12.
8. Stewart, 2006, 82.
9. Buckingham and Coffman, 1999; Peters, 1994; Stewart, 2006, 82, 84; Peters, 2008.
10. Barth, 1989, 246–247.
11. National Policy Board for Educational Administration, 1993, 18–25; Commonwealth of Massachusetts Education Laws and Regulations 603 CMR 35.00, Evaluation of Teachers and Administrators.
12. Sergiovanni, 1991, 328.

13. Sergiovanni, 1992, 32.
14. Vaill, 1989, 114.
15. Mojkowski and Bamberger, 1991, 26.
16. Hersey and Blanchard, 1988.
17. Sergiovanni, 1992, 33.
18. Pittenger, 1993; Carskadon and Cook, 1982; and McRae and Costa, 1989.
19. Forer, 1949.
20. Badaracco and Ellsworth, 1989, 6.
21. Ibid., 202–205.
22. "The Wizard of Oz." Wikipedia.
23. Vaill, 1984, 102.

2. They'll Never Understand

1. Malkiel, 1990, 25.
2. Bennis and Nanus, 1985, 21.
3. Bolman and Deal, 1991, 29.
4. Mintzberg, 1989, 3.
5. Bennis, 1989, 15–16.
6. Morgan, 1986, 180–181.
7. Jones, 1994, 27.
8. Colb, personal communication, July 29, 2009.

3. Change Is What It Means

1. Bennis, 1989, 20–21.
2. Marris, 1986, 5.
3. Gould, 1991, 60.
4. Marris, 6.
5. Marris, 10–11.
6. Vaill, 1989, 57.
7. Schein, 1987, 92–94; 1985, 252–256, 294–295; 1992, 298–303; 1993, 88–90.
8. Fullan, 1991, 91.
9. Marris, 21.
10. Marris, 158.

11. Shahan, personal communication, February 16, 2009.
12. Fullan, 127.
13. Marris, 155.
14. Schein, 1987, 98.
15. Fullan, 91.

4. Bite Off What You Can Chew

1. Drucker, 1976, 24.
2. Csikszentmihalyi, 1995, 107.
3. Gallagher, 1998, 60, 43.
4. Barton and Coley, 1992.
5. Vaill, 1984, 86.
6. Badaracco and Ellsworth, 1989, 119.
7. Hammer and Champy, 1994, 149–150.
8. Kouzes and Posner, 1987, 20.
9. Vaill, 1984, 96.
10. Kouzes and Posner, 1987, 227–228.

5. Be Your Best, Bold Self

1. Bennis, 1989, 21.
2. Vaill, 1989, 52.
3. Mintzberg, 1994, 108.
4. Ibid., 108–110.
5. Lohr, 1994, 1.
6. Schlechty, 1990, 102.

6. Nourish to Flourish

1. Kouzes and Posner, 2003, 293.
2. Eden, 1990, 171.
3. Herzberg, 1987.
4. Herzberg, 112–113.
5. Mitchell and Peters, 1988, 75.
6. Eden, 186–187.
7. Barth, 1991, 30.

7 From Savvy to Wise: Look Out for Number One

1. Chapin, 1972.
2. James, 1890, 297.
3. Reich, 1996.
4. Darling, personal communication, May 4, 2009.
5. Babcock, 1998, 1.
6. Eliot, 1952, 145.
7. Miller, 1957, 25.

References

Babcock, Mike. "I Wish My Mom Were Here." *Oak Tree Times*. Polytechnic School, 1998, 1.

Badaracco, Joseph L., and Richard Ellsworth. *Leadership and the Quest for Integrity*. Boston: Harvard Business School Press, 1989.

Barth, Roland S. "The Principal and the Profession of Teaching," in Thomas J. Sergiovanni and J. H. Moore (eds.), *Schooling for Tomorrow: Directing Reforms to Issues That Count*. Boston: Allyn & Bacon, 1989, 227–250.

Barth, Roland. *Improving Schools from Within*. San Francisco: Jossey-Bass, 1991.

Barton, Paul, and Richard J. Coley. *America's Smallest School: The Family*. Princeton: Educational Testing Service Policy Information Center, 1992.

Bennis, Warren. *Why Leaders Can't Lead*. San Francisco: Jossey-Bass, 1989.

Bennis, Warren, and Burt Nanus. *Leaders: The Strategies for Taking Charge*. New York: Harper and Row, 1985.

Bolman, Lee G., and Terrence E. Deal. *Reframing Organizations*. San Francisco: Jossey-Bass, 1991.

Buckingham, Marcus, and Curt Coffman. *First, Break All the Rules: What the World's Greatest Managers Do Differently*. New York: Simon and Schuster, 1999.

Carskadon, T. G., and D. D. Cook. "Validity of MBTI Descriptions as Perceived by Recipients Unfamiliar with Type." *Research in Psychological Type*, 1982, *5*, 89–94.

Chapin, Harry. "Greyhound." *Heads & Tales*. Elektra Entertainment Group. EKS 75023. 1972. Used by permission.

Collins, Jim. *Good to Great: Why Some Companies Make the Leap . . . and Others Don't*. New York: HarperCollins, 2001.

Csikszentmihalyi, Mihaly. "Education for the Twenty-First Century." *Daedalus*, 1995, *124*(4), 107–114.

Drucker, Peter F. *The Effective Executive*. New York: Harper and Row, 1976.

Eden, Dov. *Pygmalion in Management*. Lexington, MA: Heath, 1990.

Eliot, T. S. "Little Gidding," in *Four Quartets. The Complete Poems and Plays 1909–1950*. New York: Harcourt, Brace & World, 1952. Used by permission.

Evans, Robert. *The Human Side of School Change: Reform, Resistance, and the Real-life Problems of Innovation*. San Francisco: Jossey-Bass, 1996.

Evans, Robert. "The Authentic Leader: Surviving and Thriving in Difficult Times," in Matthew King (ed.), *Partners in Progress: Strengthening the Superintendent-Board Relationship*. New Directions for School Leadership, Jossey-Bass, 1999. 75–82.

Evans, Robert. *Family Matters: How Schools Can Cope with the Crisis in Childrearing*. San Francisco: Jossey-Bass, 2004.

Forer, Bertram R. "The Fallacy of Personal Validation: A Classroom Demonstration of Gullibility." *Journal of Abnormal and Social Psychology*, 1949, *44*, 118–123.

Fullan, Michael, with Suzanne Stiegelbauer. *The New Meaning of Educational Change*. New York: Teachers College Press, 1991.

Gallagher, James. "Education, Alone, Is a Weak Treatment."

Education Week, July 8, 1998, 60: 43.

Gould, Stephen Jay. *Bully for Brontosaurus*. New York: Norton, 1991.

Hammer, Michael, and James Champy. *Reengineering the Corporation*. New York: HarperBusiness, 1994.

Hersey, Paul, and Kenneth H. Blanchard. *Management of Organizational Behavior*. Englewood Cliffs, NJ: Prentice Hall, 1988.

Herzberg, Frederick. "One More Time: How Do You Motivate Employees?" *Harvard Business Review*, September-October 1987, 5–16.

James, William. *Principles of Psychology*. New York: Holt, 1890.

Jones, Rebecca. "The Loneliness of Leadership." *Executive Educator*, March 1994, 26–30.

Kouzes, James M., and Barry Z. Posner. *The Leadership Challenge*. San Francisco: Jossey-Bass, 1987.

Kouzes, James M., and Barry Z. Posner. *The Jossey-Bass Academic Administrator's Guide to Exemplary Leadership*. San Francisco: Jossey-Bass, 2003.

Lohr, Steve. "On the Road with Chairman Lou." *New York Times*, June 26, 1994, Sect. 3.

Malkiel, Burton G. *A Random Walk Down Wall Street*. New York: Norton, 1990.

Marris, Peter. *Loss and Change*. London: Routledge & Kegan Paul, 1986.

McRae, R. R., and Costa, P. T. "Reinterpreting the Myers-Briggs Type Indicator from the Perspective of the Five-Factor Model of Personality." *Journal of Personality*, 1989, 57(1), 17–40.

Miller, Henry. *Big Sur and the Oranges of Hieronymus Bosch*. New York: New Directions, 1957.

Mintzberg, Henry. "Planning of the Left Side, Managing on the Right," in *Mintzberg on Management*. New York: Free Press, 1989, 43–55.

Mitchell, Douglas E., and Martha Jo Peters. "A Stronger Profession Through Appropriate Incentives." *Educational Leadership*, 1988, 46(3), 74–78.

Mojkowski, Charles, and Richard Bamberger. *Developing Leaders for Restructuring Schools: New Habits of Mind and Heart.* Washington, DC: National LEADership Network, 1991.

Morgan, Gareth. *Images of Organization.* Beverly Hills: Sage, 1986.

National Policy Board for Educational Administration. *Principals for Our Changing Schools: Knowledge and Skill Base.* Fairfax, VA: National Policy Board for Educational Administration, 1993.

Paul, Annie Murphy. "I Feel Your Pain." *Forbes,* December 27, 2004. www.forbes.com/forbes/2004/1227/038.html. Retrieved March 31, 2009.

Peters, Tom. *The Pursuit of Wow!* New York: Vintage, 1994.

Peters, Tom. Author's Q & A re: *The Circle of Innovation: You Can't Shrink Your Way to Greatness.* Vintage, 1999. www .randomhouse.com/vintage/catalog/display.pperl?isbn= 9780679757658&view=qa. Retrieved April 8, 2008.

Pittenger, David J. "Measuring the MBTI . . . and Coming Up Short." *Journal of Career Planning and Employment,* 1993, 54(1), 48–52.

Reich, Robert. "My Family Leave Act." *New York Times,* November 8, 1996.

Resnick, Bruce G., and Timothy L. Smunt. "From Good to Great to . . ." *The Academy of Management Perspectives,* 22(4), 2008, 6–12.

Schein, Edgar. *Organizational Culture and Leadership.* San Francisco: Jossey-Bass, 1985.

Schein, Edgar. *Process Consultation Vol. II.* Reading, MA: Addison-Wesley, 1987.

Schein, Edgar. *Organizational Culture and Leadership.* 2nd ed. San Francisco: Jossey-Bass, 1992.

Schein, Edgar. "How Can Organizations Learn Faster? The Challenge of the Green Room." Sloane Management Review,Winter, 1993, 85-92.

Schlechty, Phillip C. *Schools for the 21st Century.* San Francisco: Jossey-Bass, 1990.

Sergiovanni, Thomas J. *The Principalship: A Reflective Practice Perspective.* Boston: Allyn & Bacon, 1991.

Sergiovanni, Thomas J. *Moral Leadership: Getting to the Heart of School Reform*. San Francisco: Jossey-Bass, 1992.

Stewart, Matthew. "The Management Myth." *Atlantic Monthly*, 2006, 297(5), 80–87.

Tannenbaum, Robert, and Warren H. Schmidt. "How to Choose a Leadership Pattern," in *Managers as Leaders*, Harvard Business Review Paperback No. 90084. Cambridge, MA: Harvard Business Review, [1957] 1991.

Thomson, Scott D. "Leadership Revisited." *Education Week*, Oct. 16, 1991.

Vaill, Peter B. "The Purposing of High-Performing Systems," in Thomas J. Sergiovanni and John E. Corbally (eds.), *Leadership and Organizational Culture*. Urbana: University of Illinois Press, 1984, 85–104.

Vaill, Peter B. *Managing as a Performing Art*. San Francisco: Jossey-Bass, 1989.

"The Wizard of Oz." Wikipedia.
http://en.wikipedia.org/wiki/
The_Wizard_of_Oz_(1939_film). Retrieved May 9, 2008.

Index